T

Value Of

Political Capit$l

Dennis A. DiZoglio

LP

Printed in the United States of America

First Printing, 2018

ISBN 978-0-931507-47-2

Loom Press Publishing
P.O. Box 1394
Lowell, Massachusetts 01853

978-454-4883

www.loompress.com

Dedication

This book is dedicated to my wife Barbara and my daughters, Sara and Rebecca who provided the support, sensitivity and understanding to allow me to do the things I wanted to do with my life even though it may have taken away time I might have shared with them. Thanks for being there when I needed you. Love Always!

Contents

Introduction

I have worked in local and regional government for over 35 years. As a trained public administrator, I know how public policy is developed and implemented. As a practitioner I also have experienced how it actually works and more over how it does not work. I had the privilege of serving as the elected Mayor of Methuen, Massachusetts for 6 years, a City with over 42,000 people and a municipal budget of over $100 million dollars. During that tenure the merging of the academic and real life experiences happened frequently. I decided that the clashing of disciplines was a good story so I decided to write a book on my experiences. Here it is.

When I decided to write the book, I thought hard as to the kind of book I wanted to write. I did not want to do an autobiography since my story is not what I believe to be the most interesting part of my experiences. Yet explaining how government works and doesn't work would benefit from understanding what motivated my career, how I came to power, and telling that story is important.

I did not want to write a "tell all" book since I believe that my experiences are transferable to the greater business of running a government. While the experiences I had involve specific individuals, the stories are universal and could be the same no matter what community or level of government is examined.

I did not want to write a political science book since there are a number of books and articles that currently exist that attempt to describe the academic elements of policy development, leadership and politics. The merging of the story and the theory is what I find interesting and what I believe is worth telling.

So the book will be a hybrid or a mix of approaches. The early part of the book will focus on my life and the influences that molded me into the person I am. It will also deal with how my career evolved and advanced, how I prepared for this rewarding life, and how I used my skills to get elected as Mayor of Methuen.

The subsequent chapters will not focus on the chronology of my career but more on the responsibilities, leadership and relationship dynamics that are inherent in government. I will pay particular attention to the responsibilities of the participants in the process such as the city council. City councilors often perceive their role much differently than what a city charter prescribes, which creates an inherit clash of roles between them and the mayor.

I will also discuss how to use your control over the agenda to manage and move the government forward. A mayor must stay focused on a manageable agenda and use their "Political Capital" to get things done.

I will also discuss that in some instances events allow leaders to rise above just managing the bureaucracy and to make government effective, responsive and relevant. You have heard people say that a person "is a born leader" but it takes a crisis to really allow someone to exhibit that skill.

I will explore how the public; volunteers and the press interact with the government and affect public policy development and implementation. The day to day work of the government is a people business. You need to be able to have "people skills" to be successful and make government work.

I will also discuss how the structure of the government can influence relationships and that sometimes this can lead to an ineffective and inefficient government. Organizational charts and city charters are boring to folks but at the end of the day how the government is structured and operates can be the difference between success and failure.

Also discussed will be how the public expects more from public officials than what is outlined in a city charter. When you are mayor you are the leader of the community and your responsibilities sometimes go beyond what is required or allowed by law.

Not all elected officials have term limits. In fact, most do not, but the impact term limits have on governing is something I experienced and the story is worth talking about. In the end the job of mayor is very rewarding and if done right a great deal can be accomplished.

All of these topics will be discussed with the use of stories and anecdotes that pose questions about the effectiveness of government and in some cases, suggest what public officials can expect and how they can prepare themselves for success. I hope this book will slide the curtain back just a little and show the reader what it is like being an elected and appointed official in government today.

I have tried to recreate events, locales and conversations from my memories of them. I have made every effort to not represent anyone's opinion and used newspaper articles, which have been footnoted, to ensure that the information in this book was correct at press time. If anyone mentioned in the book feels that I have misrepresented their opinions or position please let me know and I will attempt to correct the misunderstanding. I do not assume and hereby disclaim any liability to any party for any pain or suffering I caused by writing this book or by errors or omissions, whether such errors or omissions resulted from negligence, accident, or any other cause

Chapter 1

"Who Am I? Why Am I Here?"(1)

Between 1940 and 1960 the City of Lawrence Massachusetts lost over 25,000 textile jobs. (2) Considering the population in 1950 was 80,000 residents that was a significant loss to the local economy. As you can imagine growing up in a community that was undergoing drastic changes influenced my life.

Lawrence was developed as a planned industrial city in 1844. The 7.4 square miles of land was strategically located along the Merrimack River and the "Great Stone Dam" was constructed to harness the river to drive the community's development. Lawrence was one of the first cities in New England that spawned the birth of the US industrial revolution.

Over 13 million square feet of industrial mill buildings were constructed in Lawrence along the Merrimack River. One of the largest mill complexes was the Wood Mill, which was comprised of twin mill buildings that housed over 2.5 million square feet of space. While one of the buildings was demolished to make parking available to stimulate the use of the remaining building the sheer size of the building dominates the landscape. If you place the Wood Mill on its end it would be higher than the Empire State Building, in New York City.

Surrounding these many mill complexes were neighborhoods of immigrants eager to work in the mill buildings. Each ethnic group formed its own neighborhood and anchored the neighborhood with religious institutions. The Irish constructed St. Mary's and St. Lawrence O'Toole Churches in North Lawrence and St. Patrick's Church in South Lawrence. The Italians constructed Holy Rosary Church, the French Canadians constructed St. Anne's Church and Sacred Heart Church, the Polish settled around the Holy Trinity Church and the Jews had two synagogues on Tower Hill. To add to the mix the Yankee farmers developed neighborhoods around Congregational and Episcopalian churches. Lawrence was a true melting pot for all these groups and growing up and experiencing all the differences enriched the experience.

When I was born we lived with my father's mother and father on North Lowell Street next to the First Congregational Church and across the Common from the Holy Rosary Grammar School, which was part of the Italian neighborhood. My father had left school early and never graduated from high school. He left to work in the textile mills to help support the family. He was a weaver but had the ambition to be more than a mill worker. He enlisted in the Navy toward the end of World War II. When he returned he married, started a family and looked for more opportunities

He worked for his brother who had a painting company and learned the painting trade. Shortly thereafter he struck out on his own as a painting contractor going door to door offering his services. He also approached oil companies who were trying to do business with consumers who were part of America's love affair with the automobile. The oil companies like Texaco, Mobile, Shell, Getty and CITGO owned hundreds of gas service stations in New England and he developed relationships with these companies and began painting their stations. With his business starting to prosper he bought a two-family house on Prospect Hill and moved the family out of my grandfather's house. The neighborhood was comprised of two and three family houses with a mix of ethnicities just outside the industrial area on the north side of the River. I remember every morning seeing our Studebaker station wagon littered with soot and ash left from the Oxford Paper Mill manufacturing process the night before.

My mother quit her job as a stitcher in the mills when the business started to prosper to help run the business and keep the books. My father's ambition expanded his efforts into real estate development and he began to purchase and construct multifamily homes and complexes throughout the city. At one point he had over sixty units of housing in his portfolio. My mother and father were living the American dream and my sisters and I had a front row seat watching this fairy tale come true. As the oldest sibling and the only male, I was a little closer to the action working with my father every summer while in high school and college. Swinging a brush and working as a professional painter was hard and dirty work but we could see the rewards. My father was so successful that he retired at 55 years of age. Not bad for a person without a high school education.

Being part of the American dream and growing up in a declining American city influenced me and molded me into the person I am today. The first thing I learned was that hard work and perseverance can lead to success. I saw the long hours and hard work my parents put into the business, which led to success. When I worked with my father I was often tired at the end of a long day but felt a sense of accomplishment each and every day when the job was done. Most people from Lawrence worked hard to get ahead. Many became successful and actually moved out of Lawrence and into the surrounding suburbs as a sign of being successful, which in some ways contributed to the city's decline. Seeing and experiencing this approach in life influenced me greatly. A strong work ethic and ambition has driven my career.

The second way this environment I grew up in influenced me was in the choice for a career. When you talk with any former Lawrencian who grew up during this time frame they will undoubtedly speak fondly of the lifestyle they had and lament how it changed and deteriorated and drove them to leave their hometown. We will talk about how Essex Street in downtown Lawrence was the retail center for the region. All Lawrencians and residents of the surrounding communities would come to downtown Lawrence and shop, dine and recreate. We will all tell you how we would walk downtown, shop at Mack's or Duke's for cloths and purchase our fine clothing items at Kap's, McCartney's, Gentry's or Cherry and Web's. We will talk about how we had Lebanese food at Bishop's or Italian food at Savastano's and bought pastries at Melville's, Pappy's and Fisichelli's. How we went to the movies at The Palace, The Star, The Warner and The Broadway Theater and how we bowled at the Rec both candlepin and duck pin and played billiards. And how we shopped at Sears and Roebucks and Woolworths and finished up with banana splits at the counter. They will also talk about how their grandparents and mothers and fathers worked in the textile mills and what it was like growing up in diverse and ethnic neighborhoods and going to church dances.

All those establishments are gone now. It took years for it to happen. Every year one or two of these cherished activities would be gone. Retail establishments in the downtown closed or moved to the suburban malls being constructed throughout the region. Mills became vacant or underutilized. Houses were left abandoned or deteriorated. Streets, sidewalks and parks went unrepaired. Public buildings were deteriorating and not meeting the demands of the citizenry. When your community is changing before your eyes you wonder. "Why is this happening"? "What can be done to reverse this trend"? "Who is responsible for addressing these issues"? Even as a young boy I recognized and believed that it was government that had the responsibility to address these issues and create the best possible place for people to bring up their families and provide for their welfare in their pursuit for happiness.

When I was growing up the government was dominated by Irish politicians who served as mayor. But the form of government in the city provided opportunities for the other ethnic groups to participate. The City of Lawrence at that time had a unique form of government known as the "Commission Form". It was first enacted in Galveston, Texas (3) to respond to a natural disaster and called for an elected mayor, who is part of the city council, and a city council comprised of four aldermen who were elected to manage a portion of the government. The mayor was chairperson of the council and was responsible for all the finances in the city, prepared the budget and was the face of the government. The alderman of public safety managed the police and fire functions of the city. The alderman of park and recreation managed the parks, playgrounds, pools and other recreational activities. The alderman of engineering managed the department of public works activities and the alderman of health and welfare managed the welfare entitlements (eliminated when the State took over the function), the health department and trash pickup and disposal. Many of these elected positions were held by people from other ethnic groups in the city.

This unique form of government was not very efficient or effective. The city council itself became an area where politics was supreme. Since the mayor controlled the budget the alderman found it difficult to provide the checks and balances intended from the city council. And the council's relationship between themselves and the mayor was "you scratch my back I will scratch your back". There was no sharing of equipment or personnel and the government acted more like five separate entities. In this form of government, the role that struck me as the most important was the mayor. The mayor set the agenda and controlled the political power to advance the agenda. While clearly the leader of the community the mayor was very limited because of the fragmented nature of the government but it still made me think that this was the kind of position that could make a difference.

No one aspires to be mayor without some career path to follow. Since there is uncertainty associated with how one's career will unfold and whether there will even be an opportunity to be elected a mayor you need to choose a path that motivates you. As I watched my community change before my eyes it made me want to find a career that would allow me to help reverse this direction. When you consider a discipline that deals predominately with community revitalization it leads you to planning and community development. With this in mind I charted a career path to accomplish this direction.

I majored in political science at Merrimack College and received the degree of Master in Public Administration from Suffolk University. My initial professional positions began in 1979 and were in the field of economic development for the City of Lawrence. My responsibilities included neighborhood revitalization and business development. Although it was the conditions in Lawrence that led me to this career field I found my ambition motivated me to look for opportunities to lead my own department. This first opportunity was to become the Director of Planning and Economic Development for the City of Taunton, Massachusetts in 1984. It was a newly created department that was formed to combine the urban renewal efforts of the community, previously managed by the Taunton Redevelopment Authority (TRA), with the planning and economic development agenda of the city. I developed an organizational chart for the new department and staffed the department. Besides coordinating the permitting functions of the city, the new department sought after and received Community Development Block Grant (CDBG) funding to continue the community's revitalization efforts and began to market and develop the Miles Standish Industrial Park created by the city.

The next opportunity came with my appointment as the Community Development Director for the City of Peabody, Massachusetts in 1986. Under the auspices of the community development department the city placed its planning, permitting, development and revitalization functions. The disposition of land in Centennial Industrial Park and the development and management of an action plan for the use of over $8M in Urban Development Action Grants (UDAG) awarded to the city to stimulate the creation and development of Centennial Industrial Park, which was funded in part by the Economic Development Administration (EDA), was also the responsibility of the Community Development Department. Unlike the City of Taunton, the city used the department for its capital improvement planning and implementation. I was responsible for the planning and building of a number of new public facilities for the city, including a branch library, fire station and senior citizens center.

In 1993, I was elected the mayor of the City of Methuen, Massachusetts and was sworn in on January 3rd of 1994, fulfilling my childhood dream. Leading a community with over 42,000 people is a challenging position and is the basis for the vast majority of the experiences sighted in this book. My previous experience in government was the key to managing a multifaceted local government. Methuen is a suburb of Lawrence and shares a border with Lawrence and the State of New Hampshire, which creates its own set of challenges. Methuen, 24 square miles in size, is shaped like a butterfly, with the body of the butterfly abutting Lawrence. This section of Methuen is also comprised of downtown and the majority of the housing stock was built prior to World War II. The wings of the butterfly-shaped community, which includes the newer housing stock built post World War II, experienced significant growth in the 1980s and 1990s. Because of this growth the population of Methuen in 2010 was over 48,000.

The position of mayor was created through a charter change in 1993. This newly created position presented a vast amount of new challenges that needed to be addressed. The first of which was transitioning to the new form of government but also included the management of growth, inadequate municipal facilities, a deteriorating commercial base inhibited due to sales tax free New Hampshire, deferred maintenance and political discourse.

After serving six years as mayor I left Methuen due to term limits. The new charter set a limit of three two-year terms and after being reelected twice it was time to leave. I found my next challenge as Director of Planning for the Massachusetts Bay Transportation Authority (MBTA) the 5th largest transit agency in the United States. I was responsible for all capital planning at the MBTA and my role was expanded after being appointed Chair of the Boston Metropolitan Planning Organization (MPO) by the Massachusetts Secretary of Transportation. The MPO plans and programs all federal transportation dollars coming into the Boston region, which is comprised of 101 cities and towns. The MPO needed to prioritize projects and build consensus around the decisions on which projects should be programmed. Before I left the MBTA, seven years later, I rose to the position of Deputy General Manager for Planning and Development and managed all planning functions for the MBTA. I was also responsible for the management and sale of all real estate in the MBTA portfolio. The MBTA is the second largest landholder in the State of Massachusetts. The State itself is the largest land holder in Massachusetts. A significant effort was to sell properties to raise revenue for the MBTA and to encourage Transit Oriented Development (TOD) around transit stations.

In 2007, I was appointed the Executive Director of the Merrimack Valley Planning Commission (MVPC). MVPC was created in 1959 to "promote cooperation and coordination and the orderly development of the region". The Merrimack Valley Region is comprised of fifteen-member communities (Amesbury, Andover, Boxford, Georgetown, Groveland, Haverhill, Lawrence, Methuen,

Merrimac, Newbury, Newburyport, North Andover, Rowley, Salisbury and West Newbury) with over 270 Square Miles of area and over 335,000 residents. The Valley is located in the northeast quadrant of Massachusetts along the New Hampshire border. The Commission accomplishes its mission with the use of multi-dimensional planning disciplines. The disciplines include: transportation, land use, economic development, and environmental and is supported by an innovative Geographic Information Technology (GIS) group. In 2007, I helped form the Merrimack Valley Mayors and Managers Coalition, which was formed to identify common challenges the communities faced and to consider ways they could work together to meet those challenges. The coalition is comprised of the five cities (Amesbury, Haverhill, Lawrence, Methuen and Newburyport) and three towns with strong town managers (Andover, North Andover and Salisbury). MVPC provides the administrative support for the coalition. I retired in 2016 and decided to share my experiences through this book.

Chapter 2

"Win Rocky Win"

In 1978, the Methuen Charter was revised to have a town manager and a town council with nine councilors. The councilors were elected with three members elected at large and two members elected from each of the three districts, west, east and central. In 1984, a citizen petition was placed on the ballot to change the Town of Methuen Charter to replace the town manager and have an elected mayor. The referendum was defeated by a two to one margin.

Once again, in 1993 a citizen petition was placed on the ballot to change the Town of Methuen Charter to replace the town manager and have an elected mayor. The referendum was approved by a two to one margin, 4,172 to 2,109. So, what changed in just ten years? The short answer is Mike McLaughlin was appointed Methuen Town Manager in 1990. According to the *Lowell Sun*, McLaughlin had a checkered past. Early in his career he was an elected state representative from Billerica and was investigated by the district attorney's office for allegedly pressuring Billerica businesses to make donations to his campaign. In 1976, he was appointed to the Middlesex County Commission, which oversees the county court, jail and work-release programs. He pleaded the Fifth Amendment 71 times before a grand jury that was investigating the hiring of relatives of reputed Boston mobsters for county jobs(4).

McLaughlin was selected to be the Lowell Housing Authority (LHA) Director in 1986. In 1987, he became the focal point of a questionable lobbying effort while vying for the Lowell City Manager job. State police wiretaps caught reputed Lowell bookie Jackie McDermott having multiple phone conversations with McLaughlin and trying to line up councilor votes on McLaughlin's behalf. He did not get the City Manager job.

By 1990, LHA board members, citing McLaughlin's political strong-arming tactics, bought out the remainder of his contract. Despite these controversies the Methuen Town Council appointed him as their town manager in 1990. From there, McLaughlin entered a stormy two-year employment as Methuen's Town Manager.

Speaking about McLaughlin in 1990, Senator and future Presidential candidate Paul Tsongas was quoted as saying, "In all my life in politics, from the Lowell City Council to the U.S. Senate, no one worries me more than Michael McLaughlin."(4)

Town officials and residents were frequently at odds with McLaughlin regarding his "style of government." The town council decided not to renew his three-year contract, and he resigned his position. The citizens began their referendum effort to move away from an appointed town manager to an elected mayor and in April of 1993 the referendum was approved.

At first when the charter was changed I did not consider running for the position. My career was going well. I was not well known in the community and my last name is not the easiest to pronounce. Obviously because of my childhood interest in being a mayor I did not totally rule out a run, but I was definitely not a candidate initially.

The charter change referendum called for a primary election to be held on October 5th with a final election to be held in November. Shortly after the vote in May candidates started to emerge. As you can imagine some of the candidates were existing city councilors interested in taking the mayor's position. While they were familiar with the city and its issues, many of them lacked experience in actually managing a community. Their primary occupations were in fields outside of government. There was an electrician, a self-employed investment councilor and the owner of a local liquor store. Other candidates who were not elected officials similarly lacked government experience. The occupations for some of the other candidates included: flight attendant, teacher, janitor, police officer, owner of a sports cards store and a local lawyer. Even McLaughlin was reported in a local newspaper as considering a run.

I firmly believe that what the voters were saying with their support for the mayor form of government was that they wanted to see some professionalism and credibility returned to their government and the best way to do that was to elect a mayor who had the right experience and would be accountable to them. By July there were ten candidates announced for mayor and I began to feel that my experience would best meet what the citizens wanted.

Up to this point my life had been private. I lived in Methuen but commuted to Peabody Monday through Friday to work. My wife and I were raising a family and we were very involved in our daughters' lives. I told my wife of my interest in running for mayor and it was not well received. My wife felt that our lives would be disrupted significantly. While I was now out many nights due to public meetings the thought of our lives being up front and public was not part of what she hoped for us. Over the course of a few weeks, I continued to raise the issue and heard the same reservations. As corny as it sounds I received a call from my wife at work on Monday July 12th. When I answered the phone she said, "Win Rocky Win"(5). Being fans of the movie, I immediately knew what she meant and I announced my candidacy on July 14th. I was the last candidate to file nomination papers.

An article in the local newspaper, *The Eagle Tribune*, announcing my candidacy outlined my career up to that point and my desire to bring professionalism and credibility to the position. Having never run for political office before and having only family and friends in the community I was certainly at a disadvantage to someone who wanted to be mayor. The day after my announcement was reported in the paper I received a call from a sitting City Councilor, Joe Pappalardo, a leader in the charter change referendum effort and he asked if I would be interested in meeting with some Methuen folks about my candidacy. I jumped at the chance and I invited them over my house to discuss the issues. There were about fifteen people who attended the meeting, a mix of elected councilors and citizens, who had one thing in common, they were supporters of the charter change and were looking for a candidate that could instill confidence in Methuen's government. Since the cornerstone of my campaign was touting my experience I handed out my resume and reviewed it with them. They asked why I was interested in running for Mayor. I told them that as residents of Methuen, my wife and I would consistently hear "Methuen is a nice place to live but..." and the "but" would always lead to a discussion of Methuen's raucous local government. I told them that "I have worked in government and know you can make the government more accountable and trusted and that was what drove me to run."

The next day I was called and told the group was on board. Ken Bourassa and Jim Bamford, who attended the meeting and were active participants in previous local campaigns offered to be my campaign managers. Bamford had taken the resume I had distributed to the group and went down to the local printers and had hundreds of copies made on fluorescent yellow paper and my first campaign literature was born.

When distributing the resume people would say "hey check this out this guy has the experience and he is not a politician." My resume was somewhat crude in its delivery but the use of it led to our campaign slogan "A Professional not a Politician".

When I decided to run I vowed to run a credible and competitive campaign. I was not going to disrupt my life and spend countless hours in an effort that I could not look back on and say I gave it my best shot. Through the years I have seen many candidates decide to run for a political office and fail to mount an effective campaign or put sufficient effort into the run. Maybe many of them felt that the name on the ballot gives people the opportunity to vote for them and through their family and friends that will be enough, but it is rarely the case. Why should a person vote for an individual? The candidate needs to make the case if they want to win. Now some voters may decide to vote for someone as a protest to the other candidate(s) or to send a message to an incumbent, but for the most part you need to tell the voter why you.

There are some exceptions when voters decide to send a message. Usually an incumbent makes a decision or has done something that the electorate is not too keen on and decides to send a message to the incumbent that "I know you are going to win, but I want to let you know that I am not totally satisfied". For example, in 2001 the City of Beverly, Massachusetts elected Thomas Crean Mayor by just 245 over the eight-year incumbent Bill Scanlon. Crean had not campaigned significantly, but won because voters were sending a message to the incumbent that police department promotions and irregularities didn't sit well with them. Two year later Scanlon was elected by 6,250 votes to Crean's 4,356 (6)-the protest was over.

Because of the Methuen Charter change there was no incumbent in the field so there was no protest vote. Each candidate had to tell the voters what made them the best option. Some relied on family and friends and thought a campaign that stressed name recognition was a good strategy. It is not! In the beginning of the campaign I was driving down East Street one of the main streets through Methuen and noticed dozens of Mullen for Mayor Signs, one of the mayoral candidates. My immediate thought was I was in deep trouble. How am I going to compete with that kind of support and recognition? I soon learned that signs do not vote and along with visibility you need to have a campaign strategy if you want to get elected. Mullin's father was the grand knight at the Methuen Knights of Columbus and with his connections secured these sign locations for his son. When the primary vote came in Mullin received 159 votes out of 10,500 votes cast and came in tenth out of eleven candidates. In the end he received fewer votes than the number of signs he had posted throughout the community.

Another strategy used is to go negative against your opponents. There has been significant debate on the effectiveness of negative campaigning. While the research in non-conclusive a comprehensive literature analysis published in 2007 in the *Journal of Politics* examined the effects of political ads. The authors reported that negative ads tended to be more memorable than positive ones but that they did not affect voter choice. People were no less likely to turn out to the polls or to decide against voting for a candidate who was attacked in an ad (7).

Some negative ads can be memorable and amusing. One of the issues raised during my campaign by my opponent was that I was not from Methuen. I grew up in Lawrence and my opponent thought it was an issue to highlight since he was a lifelong resident of Methuen. He produced two radio ads, which tried to raise the newcomer angle. In one ad a voice over was used to represent me in a cowboy and western setting and had my character ask a saloon keeper "Howdy partner I'm a stranger in town and I'm looking for town hall can you help me out." In another radio spot a police cruiser pulled my character over and issued a ticket for wandering around town and not knowing where I was going. The ads were not very effective since many residents of Methuen grew up in Lawrence and moved to Methuen.

In 2003, my successor Sharon Pollard ran for re-election against a sitting City Councilor, Todd Woekel. His campaign was negative and criticized the Mayor's patronage and awarding of contracts and had very little on what he wanted to do for Methuen. His approach was "vote for me because she is not good." I don't believe this approach is very effective.

Pollard had won reelection in 2001 with 55% of the vote down from her vote count in 1999 of 60%. In 2001 she ran against a weak candidate who raised little money and focused on one issue anti-fluoridation and Woekel perceived that Pollard had lost some of her support and decided to go negative.

After coming in second to Pollard in the preliminary election Woekel accused Pollard of being part of the "old boy network" and "rewarded friends with jobs and pay increases while ignoring the average citizen". He published a list of contributors to the Mayor's re-election campaign and tried to connect donations to patronage jobs and the awarding of city contractors to local businesses that donated to her campaign. He also accused her of using strong arm tactics with city councilors. The campaign was so negative the Eagle Tribune used the headline "Mayor's contest rancor overshadowed other races". In 2003 Pollard was reelected with 62% of the vote, 5,810 to 3,584. During her victory interview Pollard was quoted as saying "He (Woekel) only tried showing why they (voters) should not re-elect me. He did not tell people why they should elect him" (8).

Although not an incumbent I was perceived to be a front runner and was attacked for endorsements from politicians like former Senator and future Mayor Sharon Pollard and Councilor Joe Pappalardo, for allowing them to "pull the strings behind the scenes" and for being pro development since some developers had donated to my campaign. While it sounds altruistic I firmly believe that you should run for the position and not campaign negatively against your opponents. You need to develop a strategy and a campaign around telling the voter why you are the best candidate. That is exactly what we did.

I firmly believed that my "experience" factor was the key issue in the campaign, but I also felt I needed to expand on this basic strategy and begin to tell the voters what this experience would mean to them. While my first campaign piece was my resume, subsequent handouts began to outline some of the approaches I would bring to Methuen City Hall. The message I wanted to send was the need to bring credibility back to our government with true professionalism, sound fiscal management and an open government. I talked about a code of ethics for elected and appointed officials. I talked about exploring trash privatization. I talked about upgrading the educational system and building a new school. I talked about revitalizing the Arlington Neighborhood, the neighborhood abutting Lawrence with the oldest housing stock and the lowest homeownership in Methuen. I talked about stabilizing taxes through economic development as I had done in the cities I had worked in previously.

The strategy to get this message out was based on targeted mailings and personalized contact with voters. There are over 23,000 registered voters in Methuen. Recognizing it would be too expensive and too time consuming to reach all these potential voters we developed a database of active voters, those that had voted over the past four elections. All mass mailing was sent to this targeting data base. We developed different campaign pieces that highlighted my experience and priorities.

One of the most interesting pieces capitalized on me being a professional manager. We prepared a mock tear sheet of an ad one would post in a local paper for a job opening. The mock posting was titled "Wanted Mayor for the Town of Methuen". The ad outlined the qualifications for the mayor's position and required 10 years of progressive experience in government and an advanced degree. Attached to the tear sheet was a cover letter from me applying to the citizens of

Methuen to be elected their mayor. The cover letter highlighted how I met the requirements for the position, asked for their vote and was signed by me. Also attached in the envelope was my resume. They were the employer and I was the applicant for the position. The feedback from this piece was very positive. Some of the citizens even asked when the city posted the ad! Another piece centered on testimonials from mayors and other public officials I had worked with over the years. The testimonials highlighted attributes like having integrity, being professional, innovative and a problem solver and other attributes needed to be a mayor.

Personal contact with the voters took on many different looks. The initial personal approach was going door to door using the list of active voters as the target group. We developed a handout with my vision and experience for Methuen and I would hand it out to everyone that would come to the door. If the person was not at home I would leave a personal note indicating I was sorry I missed them and hoped they would review the handout, asked them to vote for me and if they had any questions to give me a call.

In neighborhoods where we had a supporter I would walk the neighborhood with them and they would introduce me to their neighbors. We also tried to organize neighborhood block parties with a supporter and have them invite their neighbors. Another personal contact approach involved sending a letter to individuals to whom I had a connection.

For example, letters were sent to all Central Catholic High School, Merrimack College and Suffolk University alumnus who lived in Methuen. I highlighted that I attended the same school they attended and that we had that in common and hoped that they would look at my qualifications and asked them to vote for me. Letters were also sent to families involved in institutions that my family was involved in as well, such as softball, gymnastics and church. Another personal contact took the form of writing each person who signed my nomination papers and asking them to vote for me.

While we did not conduct any polls during the campaign there were indications that this strategy was working. During debates the other candidates would focus on me, which clearly indicated they were hearing my name more often while they were campaigning. The citizens started to respond to my candidacy. While campaigning at a Methuen High School football game I introduced myself to a group of citizens and after asking those to consider me I left and heard one of them say to the others "he won't make it, he is too qualified".

There were other signs we were sending the right message. While going door to door I met a woman who was having a bridge party just when I arrived. She invited me in and the entire group of ladies all commented how they were hoping to meet me and I spent an hour with them talking about the issues. When I was holding signs attempting to improve my visibility folks would wave enthusiastically and even pull over to shake my hand. One woman pulled over opened her window and said, "I just have to shake your hand". When I reached in her small dog almost bit my hand off! We both had a good laugh, but I could tell the strategy was working. The night before the primary I was going door to door with a supporter in his neighborhood. Every neighbor we met that night said they were going to vote for me. At the end of the night the supporter and I looked at each other and agreed what just happened was incredible.

The next day the primary was held and I was the top vote getter with 4,300 votes out of the 10,800 votes cast or 41%. I won all twelve precincts in the community. In exit polling conducted by the reporters from the local papers, voters said they favored me because I had the experience in government, but had not held elected office. It certainly sounded like our campaign message worked. Voters were quoted as saying he is "qualified by education and job experience." "He is professional and hasn't held office in town." I voted for him "because he is educated and he does this kind of thing for a living." "I'm a first-time voter and I studied the candidates. I like what he will do for Methuen." "He made a good impression when a neighbor brought him around." "He's most qualified and experienced." I voted for him because he is "a professional". (9)

So, despite my difficult name to pronounce and my lack of political experience or connections I won the primary. The election results were a "perfect storm" (10). Those voters who supported the charter change were attracted to my candidacy because they wanted to show that there would be qualified candidates interested in running for mayor and that they could elect a qualified person. The opponents to the charter change saw a candidate who had the qualifications to be a town manager and decided to vote to continue the professional attributes inherent in a town manager form of government.

Of course, this was only the primary but the momentum of getting 41% of the vote out of 11 candidates made my chances very good that I would be elected mayor on November 2nd. My opponent was Councilor Bill Manzi who received 1,775 votes or 17% of the vote. Although the majority of other candidates endorsed Manzi in the final election, we continued to implement our campaign strategy and my message had clearly taken hold and I was elected by a 3 to 1 margin, 9,400 to 3,200.

Chapter 3

"Time to Govern"

On November 8, 1993 I was being interviewed by a reporter from the Methuen Journal regarding the transition of power and my objectives when I took office in January. Toward the end of the interview the reporter told me he looked forward to seeing me at the bi-monthly town council meetings.

I said, "Sure I will see you at the ones I decide to attend". Before I could stand up to leave the reporter said "WAIT! Are you telling me that you are not going to attend all the town council meetings?" I reminded him that we had just changed the form of government and that there is a separation of powers between the mayor and the council and that most mayors in other cities do not attend the council meeting unless his or her presence would be helpful.

On November 9th the headlines in the Methuen Journal read: "DiZoglio Says He Might Avoid Most Town Council Meetings". My comments were not off the cuff, I needed an opportunity to define the roles of the two branches of government and this was an opportunity to do so.

Before the change in the form of the government the town manager was appointed by the town council and for all practical purposes was subservient to the council or at least to five councilors if they wanted to keep their job. Methuen was known for its volatile town council. The town council never respected the separation of legislative and executive responsibilities. From 1978 when the manager/town council form was adopted until the Town went to a mayor form, very few managers fulfilled or exceeded their three-year contracts. In fact, when I completed my second term in office (four years) I was the longest serving chief executive officer Methuen ever had.

The failure of the town council to respect the different roles between the chief executive officer and the council is one of the problems that led to the change in the form of government. My interview comment was intended to start the debate on the roles of the council and the mayor. Well it certainly did as councilors began to define the roles as they saw them in the press. The council chairperson described it this way "I feel the only difference in the charter was that we changed the title from manager to mayor. I envisioned the mayor's responsibilities, per se, to attend council meetings listen to the discussion and pick up on items the council wants him to do." Others questioned how the mayor would know what the people wanted if he did not attend the council meetings, "if he is the people's employee, what kind of forum will he conduct or hold to be accountable to the people if he does not go to council meetings." Others began to understand and said he is different from a manager, "he is completely independent as far as I am concerned he can do what he wants when he wants. And others agreed, "If there was something on the agenda and I thought he should be there, I would call him and ask him to go". (11)

During the campaign I advocated for a good relationship with the council. To be honest it is a little counterintuitive to advocate for a good relationship and then suggest that I will not attend council meetings, but I firmly believed we needed to begin our relationship with a philosophical defining of our roles. The mayor is the chief administrative officer and is responsible for the day to day administration of the city government. The council has no administrative authority and does not oversee the daily operations. During the first few weeks I had a number of individual meetings with councilors and some of our discussions centered on which janitor should be assigned to various public buildings or recommendations on who should be hired to fill vacant appointed positions. Clearly the council focus should not be on such matters.

The other major role for the mayor is to set out the overall strategic direction for the city and to build consensus with the council to gain approval. Before the mayor form of government, the town manager could not play that role because he needed to keep at least five councilors happy or based on past practice lose their job. Councilors wanted to set the agenda as well as decide what jobs went to whomever or how departments would be managed. They fought over patronage and control and were not good at building consensus with their colleagues.

I think very few people thought when they changed the form of government to reduce the political squabbling that adding another politician, the mayor, would be successful, but it was. The mayor could outline a strategic plan without the threat of losing their job and could then focus on selling the approach to the council. The council has an important role in this process, but they need to recognize their given responsibilities and use them to bring checks and balances to the approval process.

The council is responsible for approving laws, ordinances, appointment and contracts to help govern the city. Think of it, the council reviews and approves the annual budget, oversees the effectiveness of programs, establishes tax rates, authorizes entering into legal contracts, borrows funds, passes ordinances and resolutions, modifies the city's charter, regulates land use through zoning laws, regulates public health and safety, exercises eminent domain powers, regulates business activities through licensing and regulations and responds to constituent needs and complaints. Talk about an important role! Yet some councilors wanted to focus on who should work where and who should be hired.

Why do some city councilors struggle with understanding their role and more importantly appreciating their role? Most people who run for council are outgoing, involved in the community, have something to say and are ambitious. Some are motivated by gain, either for personal gain or the desire to gain influence. They want to stand out in a crowd of nine councilors and satisfy their ambitions and seek to get re-elected. How do you stand out if you are one of nine votes to approve or reject an ordinance, or a budget, or confirm an appointment or a contract? Because it is difficult councilors venture into responsibilities outside their purview to gain attention or help individuals get reassigned, hired or appointed.

Councilors want to set the agenda and dictate management responsibilities. This dynamic needed to change. It did not take long for an opportunity to demonstrate the new dynamic. Each year the council needs to approve the fiscal year (FY) budget and in June of 1993 the town council approved the FY 94 budget. In November the council usually sets the property tax rate to fund the budget they approved in June based on actual growth and tax revenues. In November of 1993 the town council could not agree on a tax rate and refused to set a tax rate and tax bills could not be sent out in January of 1994 to fund the approved FY 94 budget. A delay in setting the tax rate would result in tax bills being sent out late and would require the city to borrow $6M at a cost of $160,000 in interest to meet its cash flow needs.

Although the council had approved the spending levels in the budget their decision to not fund the approved budget was clearly a political one. The councilors who ran for mayor and were defeated decided to send me a message by not approving the tax rate. While certainly inconvenient this challenge gave me an opportunity to demonstrate the new dynamic.

The first step was to take ownership of the issue and provide leadership on resolving the problem. During my inaugural address I announced a freeze on all spending except salaries and fixed costs unless personally approved by me or the town auditor (finance director) and a request to all department heads to identify potential cuts within their budgets to reduce the overall budget and reduce the tax rate request needed to fund the budget. It was my intent to come before the council and suggest a series of actions which I hope will give the council the confidence to set a tax rate.

At my first council meeting, which I obviously attended, I proposed not to fill six DPW positions in the budget, reduce overlay funds to cover tax abatements that were not needed, reduced health insurance costs through rebidding and use reserve funds, to reduce the budget by $645,000. While some councilors advocated having the new council consider the original tax rate proposal I thought it was important to set the tone and have the mayor offer a strategic plan to resolve the problem. I met with councilors and lobbied for their support of the plan.

At this first council meeting, I decided to tone down the controversy of the mayor not attending council meetings and announced I planned on attending most council meetings and at the beginning of each meeting would provide a mayor's report and offer to answer any questions the councilors may have. I also indicated that after my report and Q&A I would leave them to their meeting and deliberations. For the most part this modified attendance approach placated some of the councilors that wanted the mayor to be present at their meeting and allowed me to change the dynamic. Of course, this approach gave councilors an opportunity to grandstand at meetings. On many occasions I would provide my report, offer to answer any questions and after responding left the meeting only to be told that just after I left a councilor would say "Gee I wish the mayor was here I have a question." The *Eagle Tribune* published an editorial on January 25, 1994 indicating their support for this modified approach:

"Methuen is certainly going through some interesting changes. Newly elected Mayor Dennis DiZoglio has irritated some of Methuen's councilors by deciding not to attend most town council meetings."

"Had he a bigger ego, the new mayor might have opted to throw his weight around at council meetings, attempting to run Methuen as his personal fiefdom. He has decided instead that he does not know everything and should not be running everything."

"In his view, the town council, is the legislative branch, and has one job to do. The mayor, representing the executive branch, has another. No other mayor goes to council meetings unless it is for a specific reason. Mandatory attendance is a remnant of the old town charter."

"The town manager worked as an employee and sometimes, whipping boy of the town council. When the charter was changed, the word "mayor" replaces "town manager"... With no mayor on hand last week, the council could find little to do. The council had no one to direct questions to. The meeting lasted only an hour."

"Given the marathon pontification and finger pointing that has embarrassed the town council in past years; perhaps short meetings are not such a bad idea. We believe the mayor has the right idea here. He is an equal to and balances against the town council not a creature of it."

"There are other ways for the council to obtain and pass along information about Methuen than to haul the mayor before it every week. In fact, it seems to us councilors will have a greater opportunity to be creative and responsive to the public with their own ideas and not the mayor's as the focus of their meetings"...

"When Mr. DiZoglio failed to appear last week for a meeting the Council chairwoman noted him as AWOL. We would prefer to note him as USCS – Using Some Common Sense."

During the campaign I offered a number of initiatives I wanted to undertake as mayor. While each initiative was an important objective to me the ability to implement each and every initiative is not as simple as an announcement. Each initiative needs to be vetted and debated with the city council and the mayor may need to build consensus and gain approval to move the initiative forward. In some respects, being elected mayor is easier than moving your agenda forward.

Unfortunately, I have seen some mayors announce their intentions, send their proposal to the council and have it rejected out of hand. To illustrate here is a very simplified narrative of a potential interchange between the mayor and the city council.

Mayor: "I propose the following action..."

City Council: "Why should we support this action?"

Mayor: "Because I said so, I am the mayor"

City Council: "Sorry denied, that is not a good enough reason"

Just because you are the mayor does not mean that your proposal will be adopted by the council. The mayor needs to invest time and effort into the deliberation and to use his or her "Political Capital" to gain council support.

"Political Capital" refers to the trust, goodwill and influence a politician has with the public and other political figures. This goodwill is a type of invisible currency that politicians can use to influence decision making. A politician needs to use their credibility, in other words their good reputation by maintaining consistent policy positions and ideological views, to influence public policy. (12)

However, "Political Capital" is very sensitive to timing and overuse. Decision making is very controversial for city councilors. Any decision they make affects their ability to get re-elected and stay a city councilor and potentially run for other elected positions. Asking city councilors to approve a number of initiatives at one time is difficult. It requires them to multi-task and separate one initiative decision from another and when the decision has potential impact on their future they defer decisions or just say no to avoid making the wrong decision. When to introduce an initiative is a strategy in and of itself.

When I was the community development director for the City of Peabody I would meet with Mayor Peter Torigian on a daily basis to discuss development issues. At those daily briefing I would inform him of the status of various efforts being managed by my department and would seek his guidance as to when to initiate adoption by the council. Although many of our efforts were ready for consideration by the council the mayor would establish when such initiatives would be advanced. He was fond of saying "Dennis where going to think about it, pray about it and then make a decision". He had a big picture view of the policies important to the community and he would defer initiatives based on priorities and competing proposals and factor in the politics of the council in deciding the timing of initiating adoption consideration.

When in Peabody I did not truly understand this timing issue, but once I was elected it became very clear that it was important. Torigian was one of the longest serving Mayors in the Commonwealth, 25 years. He was very successful during his tenure because he understood how to advance public policy. I worked for him for seven years prior to being elected mayor, and it felt as if I was enrolled in mayor 101 classes.

Overuse brings another limitation to the use of "Political Capital". The mayor has many initiatives he or she would like to advance. Using "Political Capital" for every one of these initiatives would be too time consuming and create a backlash from some city councilors who may feel they are being taken advantage of and becoming somewhat of a puppet to the mayor's will. The mayor needs to prioritize initiatives and based on timing use their "Political Capital" to advance the approval process.

A mayor needs to focus their attention on a manageable agenda. Many times, a mayor's first year in office is filled with grandiose plans and an unrealistic understanding of politics. The mayor needs to control the agenda and make sure it is consistent with their vision. This applies even to outside distractions. For example, managing energy needs is a major effort by municipal leaders. One tool being used by communities is aggregating electricity purchasing power by the community to reduce energy generation costs. Many electricity brokers try to convince communities to go through the regulation approval process with the mantra "it is a no brainer", since the government and the residents in the community will see a reduction in their electricity costs.

But the decision to start this process is not "a no brainer". The approval process requires that the council mandate participation by all of its citizens unless they opt out. Change is not easy in any community and when you mandate participation, debate and public hearings can be time consuming and dominating. The mayor needs to decide if this is consistent with their agenda and worth the distraction. There may be other initiatives that are more important to advance. You need to keep the council focused on the issues that help you achieve your objectives.

One of my first council agenda items was privatizing the trash pickup and disposal. The need to prioritize this proposal was in some ways brought on by the tax rate setting debate at my first council meeting. One of the methods used to reduce the budget was to cut some DPW positions that were vacant.

This decision left the DPW undermanned. Privatization was proposed by Acting Town Manager, Donald Desantis, and a few months before I took office was rejected by the council. Desantis was the Police Chief when McLaughlin resigned and was appointed acting town manager. Desantis was well liked and had the confidence of the council. During the debate in October of 1993, the council held a public meeting where over fifty people attended and voiced their opposition to privatization. No one talked in favor. Desantis suggested that the privatization would save the city $400,000 and would not require any layoffs since the trash workers would be reassigned to other DPW departments. Many citizens questioned the suggested cost savings. The DPW union steward indicated that while he was opposed to privatization, because he felt the city would not be able to keep its promises, the trash workers were in support since they hated their jobs and wanted to get rid of the responsibilities.

While the privatization of the trash pickup was motivated by the need to increase capacity of the DPW, the financial benefits associated with privatization had to be the reason to make the change. After my analysis I was convinced that it would save the city money. However, these savings were not easily verified or transparent. When you review the city budget there are only two line-items associated with trash pickup, labor costs and the tipping fee the municipality pays for a vendor to dispose of the trash. The cost of the contract to hire a private company to pick up and dispose of the trash exceeded these two-line items. A cursory view of the budget showed privatization did not save money.

However, just below the surface of these line items where other costs that had not been considered as part of the debate. On the personnel side the benefits associated with the trash workers, like health care, pensions and other negotiated benefits needed to be considered. In fact, when added to the personnel costs this one item tipped the financial benefits in favor of privatization but there were even more personnel impacts. The highest cases of workers compensation were trash employees, trash employees hated their jobs as indicated by their union steward and sick leave use was greater than any other DPW workers, and more seasonal employees were needed to cover high absenteeism. Another cost lost in the discussion was equipment needs. The trash truck fleet was old and in need of replacement. The capital outlay to begin replacing these vehicles was significant. The maintenance cost of keeping this old feet operational was excessive and put a strain on the vehicle maintenance staff and took away from deferred maintenance for other municipal vehicles. Even the fuel to run the fleet needed to be considered in the analysis.

This analysis became the cornerstone of my discussion with city councilors. With this analysis the council voted five to four to support privatization. While successful I do think I made a tactical error in my discussions with councilors. I focused my attention on councilors who I had a working relationship. There were four councilors who were still struggling with the new form of government and I found it difficult to have conversations with them. I was frustrated when my discussions became combative and I followed a path of least resistance. But, I was wrong. I should have approached all the councilors with the hope that I might at least improve my relationship. Maurice Lariviere who was the Town Solicitor suggested I keep those councilors in the "bull pen" with the hope of gaining their support in future initiatives. He was the best city solicitor I ever worked with and he was right in this advice.

My use of "Political Capital" was not over on this issue. After the vote some citizens who had previously indicated their opposition to trash privatization started a petition drive to overturn the decision. I penned an op-ed piece for the *Eagle Tribune* alerting citizens of the pending petition and attempted to clarify some of the misconceptions the opponents were claiming. I assured citizens that there would not be any significant change in service, there would be no new restrictions to the type of trash picked up, there would be no limit on amount of trash picked up, there would be no trash fee, and I reassured them that cost savings would happen. I also reminded them that only fifteen communities out of the three hundred and fifty-one cities and towns in Massachusetts use municipal employees to pick up trash.

I ended the piece by stating "Citizens of Methuen voted for a mayoral form of government to bring accountability to the government. If the citizens decide trash pickup privatization was not the correct decision, then they can hold me accountable at the next election." The petition drive failed to get sufficient signatures to move forward.

The next transitional challenge was the development of the FY 1995 municipal budget. During one of my mayor's reports to the council I indicated that we had begun preparing my budget for their consideration for the new fiscal year. Some of the councilors bristled at the use of the words "my budget". They counted "you mean the city budget". My feeling was that since I was the mayor, and the mayor was responsible for preparing and managing the budget, that I should take on the ownership of the budget.

The budget is the primary policy document issued by a municipality. The mayor is responsible for proposing the public policy for the community and the budget is the vehicle used. I think many public officials miss the importance of the budget as a policy document. In the budget communities express their priorities. Priorities ranging from adding more police officers, to improving planning capacity, to expanding ambulance services, to expanding code enforcement, to adding recreational opportunities are all advocated for in a budget.

I was very methodical when I prepared the budget. I did not delegate the responsibility. I notified all department heads to submit their budget requests to the city auditor. The auditor organized the requests with previous year's requests as benchmarks and both of us met individually with each department head. I questioned them on each one of their line item requests and asked what they hoped to accomplish with those funds. We discussed the opportunities to add line items or expand service or reduce service and the costs associated with doing so. I then recommended to the council the amount of funds I suggested for each line item along with the department head's request, so the council could see any variances.

Traditionally the council would hold workshops on the budget and review requests. In the past the council would grill the department head regarding their request. I again changed the dynamic and presented the budget requests myself along with the city auditor. I asked the department heads to be present in the council chambers in case there were questions that I may not have the answer to but I wanted to reiterate that it was the mayor's budget.

The biggest item of contention was the request by some councilors to include in the budget funds to satisfy any contracts negotiated with the municipal unions. There were a number of reasons why I resisted this request. First the unions had been at the negotiation table for some time and we had made little progress at finding middle ground. I wanted to encourage them to become serious in the negotiation and having no funds in the budget to fund a settlement might give them an incentive. The second reason was that the amount set aside might indicate what the city would be willing to settle for and expose a negotiating position. Since the council cannot add any funds to a budget but only reduce funding the budget was approved without funds for contract settlements.

The first one hundred days of my administration was filled with different kinds of challenges. It began with my attempt to usher in a new form of government to Methuen. On my very first day in office I needed to address the destruction of a school hardwood gym floor due to a water line break at a cost of $100,000. The school superintendent and the building inspector came to my office that day and informed me of the incident. We needed to prepare specifications, identify funding and go out to bid to replace the gym floor. While it was not a difficult project to undertake I did learn you need to be prepared for the approval process. When the bids were obtained and we were ready to recommend the lowest responsible bidder I placed the contract approval on the council agenda. During the council deliberation one of the councilors asked me what material would be used to replace the floor. I was surprised by the question since we were replacing the existing hardwood floor and I leaned forward and said into the microphone "wood". As I leaned back into my chair folks began to giggle, I guess I wasn't the only one surprised by the question.

Also during the first one hundred days I worked with the council to set a tax rate for the fiscal year and to privatize the trash pickup. We formed a downtown partnership with the business community and prepared a revitalization plan. We formed an Enterprise Community Development Partnership with the City of Lawrence to bring federal resources to both communities to begin the revitalization of the Arlington neighborhoods of Methuen and Lawrence. We introduced a first-time homeowners program for the Arlington neighborhood where only 30% of the homes are owner occupied compared to 70% citywide. To improve on how our municipal employees deliver services we introduced Total Quality Management (TQM). And to improve Methuen's image we started "Methuen on the Move", a community pride campaign. What you accomplish in the first one hundred days can carry you through your first term. It creates momentum and projects an image of progress.

Chapter 4

"Leaders Are Made Not Born"

Vince Lombardi the famous football coach of the Green Bay Packers once said "Leaders are made, they are not born. They are made by hard effort, which is the price which all of us must pay to achieve any goal that is worthwhile."(13) While hard work is a key element in leadership, a leader must have strong management skills to be successful. Leaders must be able to assess and understand a problem, they need to form a game plan to resolve the problem, they need to know how to use the organization to implement the plan and they need to motivate the players in the game to perform at their best.

However, people who regularly use these skills are considered good managers and are not referred to as good leaders. What makes a good manager a leader? Crisis!

New York City was attacked on September 11, 2001 (9/11) by Islamic extremists, the twin towers were destroyed and almost 3,000 US citizens were killed. New York City Mayor Rudy Giuliani was in office for over seven years prior to 9/11 and was about to leave office when this attack took place. Prior to the attack Mayor Giuliani's approval rating was at 36%. Many of his initiatives were either rejected or failed to accomplish their intended results. However, after 9/11 his efforts to deal with the crisis resulted in him being made

Time Magazine Person of the Year and earned him an approval rating of 79%.(14)

Crisis can and does elevate a good manager and gives them an opportunity to be considered a good leader. On December 11, 1995, a fire broke out at Malden Mills one of the largest employers in Methuen. The fire was one of the worst in the State's history. Seven hundred people were at work in the factory when a boiler exploded in one of the mill buildings. The explosion was so powerful that it ruptured gas mains. The fire quickly engulfed the buildings. Employees fled into the surrounding streets. Thirty-three employees were injured with four of them critical. Fueled by chemicals and flammable materials used in textile production, the six-alarm fire gutted the mill complex. More than 200 firefighters from as far away as New Hampshire and Boston's South Shore battled 50-foot walls of flame. Strong gusty winds and temperatures near zero degrees hampered the effort to fight the fire. The fire raged out of control for much of the night, forcing nearby residents to evacuate. By morning the once busy textile complex was a scene of utter devastation. (15)

I had just picked up my daughter from basketball practice when my cell phone rang. My wife called to tell me that the fire department called the house and that I should come down to the fire as soon as possible. When I arrived, the scene was pure chaos. Emergency vehicles from the city and surrounding communities filled the streets leading to Malden

Mills. I parked my car at a church parking lot and walked up to the fire site. Just before I reached the mill I saw my neighbor, Paul Russell, who was a Massachusetts State Police Officer who had been called in to do crowd control. He told me the fire was really bad and that we were going to have our hands full. When I turned onto the street of the mill I saw the flames reaching six stories high and I knew he was right.

One of my first thoughts, did the fire department have sufficient personnel and equipment to fight the fire? During budget deliberations you always try to strike a balance between what is requested and what the community can afford and at this moment I wondered if I may have underfunded the budget. Obviously, loss of life was an immediate concern. Fortunately, no one was killed during the fire but there were many individuals that were injured. Before I could reach the command center where the Fire Chief, Ken Bourassa, was coordinating the firefighting effort I heard over a loud speaker the Fire Chief say, "find the mayor and have him call a state of emergency."

A "State of Emergency" gives the government the ability to suspend or change procedural requirements to give the government entity the flexibility to respond to a crisis. It also alerts citizens to change their normal behavior because emergency plans are being implemented. The mayor can declare such an emergency during times of natural or man-made events. I had never had the opportunity to declare a

"State of Emergency" and I am sure that if I had access to the city solicitor he would have drafted the declaration and it could have been issued to the city council and the local media but at that moment I decided to walk over to the police officer station to prevent folks from accessing the command center that I was declaring a "State of Emergency" and to inform the police chief and notify the city council and anyone who inquired.

Once I reached the command center I informed Chief Bourassa of the declaration and asked for an executive summary of the status of the crisis. After he briefed me, I asked if there was anything I could do to assist him in his efforts. He indicated that the emergency management team was in place and he would coordinate the effort.

While the corporate offices of Malden Mills are located in Lawrence the manufacturing facility, where the fire was raging, was predominately in Methuen. The Mayor of Lawrence, Mary Clair Kennedy, was at the command center along with state and local elected officials. Feeling somewhat useless watching the firefighters respond to the fire I suggested that we need to start thinking of the impacts and response to this crisis. Methuen State Senator Jim Jajuga and Lawrence State Senator John O'Brien offered to go back to my office and begin planning relief efforts. While Methuen would be the lead in addressing the crisis, the state would need to play a role in the response so I welcomed their participation. When we arrived at my city hall office, which is on the third floor, I looked out the window and although the mill was five city blocks away the fire lit up the sky. I felt a little like Nero looking over the burning of Rome.

We began brainstorming and started to develop short and long-term plans on how to address the crisis, we also compiled lists of people and state and federal agencies to call to ask for help to implement our plans. We organized our thoughts by discussing who would be affected by this crisis. The list included the general public, workers, displaced neighbors both residential and small businesses and of course what would happen to Malden Mills itself. We decided to focus our attention on four major needs: public safety, social services, jobs and training, and economic development. To delegate responsibility to address these areas I assigned each focus area with a point person.

While the firefighting was underway we were confident that the professionals at the scene would be successful in extinguishing the fire. Since the site was under the control of the fire department I asked the chief to be responsible for extinguishing the fire, along with spot fires caused by floating embers and post fire public safety issues. Under his supervision he would work with the building commissioner to evaluate the buildings structural issues, work with the police chief to secure the site and the surrounding neighborhoods, determine if any detrimental air quality issues were present and assess the impact the fire had on the fire department itself.

Two weeks before Christmas 1,700 employees would be out of work and 60 neighborhood homes had to be evacuated. The impact on those affected was disturbing. People would be offering to help and donate money to help those in need. To accept donations and to develop procedures, mechanisms and criteria for distribution of assistance I asked the United Way to coordinate the social relief effort.

At the time we were unsure if Malden Mills would be rebuilt. We did know for certain that 1,700 jobs were in jeopardy. We knew we needed to address the immediate needs associated with being unemployed and we felt that many of the employees would need to be retrained for other jobs. The Merrimack Valley Regional Employment Board (REB) was responsible for overseeing the employment and training needs of the people in the Valley. I asked the REB to coordinate the jobs and training needs.

Helping Malden Mills rebuild and helping small neighborhood businesses adversely affected by the fire needed to be a priority. Efforts to coordinate the various business assistance programs offered by the state and federal governments would not be easy. We needed someone who knew the various programs and the players that managed those programs to coordinate this effort. I asked my

Economic Development Director, Gene O'Neill to head up this effort.

We left my office around 2:30 a.m. with an outline of our focus areas and short and long-term priorities. Key personnel in our organizational structure were identified to manage our plans and it was now time to implement.

At 5 a.m. my home phone rang. It was the health director telling me that preliminary air quality test showed there were no hazardous materials in the air around the neighborhood, but it had to be confirmed by further testing. Add another item to the list and time to get back to work.

I left my house shortly after to meet with the parade of prominent politicians coming to tour the site. I met Governor Weld in the police mobile command center and thanked him for coming to Methuen. He was obviously on our list as a key player to help implement our plan. I told him of our approach and asked if he would be willing to waive the two-week waiting period of unemployment benefits for displaced workers and extending benefits beyond the 30-week limit, to work with legislative leaders to defray some of the costs associated with fighting the fire and to assign a top aide to work with us on the economic development response to the fire. I told him our legislative delegation was on board and were part of developing the plan and even offered office space at city hall for his aide to help make this request a reality. He agreed and we headed off to meet Senators

Kennedy, Kerry and Congressman Meehan who were meeting with Aaron Feuerstein, the owner of Malden Mills, in their Lawrence headquarters.

When we got to the mill floor the room was filled with employees. Feuerstein was planning to make the announcement that the mill would be rebuilt and that the employees would be paid. This was a significant announcement and clarified some of the "what ifs" we discussed in my office. When Feuerstein made the announcement, the crowd erupted in cheers. The Senators, Governor and Congressman each spoke and thanked Feuerstein for his decision and offered assistance. I was offered an opportunity to say a few words but declined, I already heard what I wanted to hear plus I thought the crowd didn't need to hear from another politician what they already knew, which was Feuerstein had saved the day by giving them hope for their jobs and their families.

The Senators and Congressman left with the promise they would reconvene in Washington and bring federal resources to help. A meeting was hosted by Senator Kennedy at his Capitol Hill office along with Senator Kerry and Congressman Meehan with the intent to coordinate how all the federal agencies could help the fire victims. In attendance were the top officials in President Clinton's administration: Secretary of Labor Richard Reich, Secretary of Housing and Urban Development Andrew Cuomo, Federal Emergency

Management Agency Director James Lee Witt, Assistant Commerce Secretary for Economic Development (EDA) Wilber Hawkins and Small Business Administration (SBA) Director Philip Lader.

Once convened Senator Kennedy called me and asked me to participate by conference call in the meeting. This was a national news story. One of the worst fires in the country with over $500M in property damage, thirty-three people injured, 1,700 workers displaced and the owner vowing to rebuild. Malden Mills was a state of the art textile manufacture that produced Polartec a fleece material for top notch retailers like L.L. Bean, Patagonia, REI and Land's End. It could have been the subject of a movie. When I answered the phone, I could literally hear photographers and news people surrounding the participants of the meeting waiting to record every word they uttered. Senator Kennedy announced who was at the meeting and assured me that they were there to help when we knew how they could be of assistance.

I thanked the Senator for convening the meeting and for those in attendance for coming. With our plan in hand I told the assembled group that we were prepared to tell them our needs. I asked Secretary Reich to make $1M in Secretary discretionary training funds available to re-train workers. I told them that we requested a waiver from the two-week waiting period for unemployment from the Governor and he was supportive and that the training funds would be needed to help re-train employees on the new computerized textile machines Malden Mills would be including in their rebuilding plans. The Secretary agreed to make funds available.

I then asked Secretary Cuomo if he could help find housing vouchers for anyone displaced from their homes because of the fire. He also agreed to work with us on helping neighbors with their housing needs. I then told Director Witt that preliminary air quality test showed no hazardous material in the neighborhood but that we could use some help securing final testing and assurances that neighborhood residents could move back into their homes. I also asked if he could help assess the Spicket River which runs through the Malden Mills site which was potentially polluted with debris from the fire. He said he would contact the EPA and help secure the necessary testing. I then asked Secretary Witt if EDA could help us look for funding to make upgrades to the infrastructure to help support the rebuilding of Malden Mills and the Secretary agreed. I then asked Director Lader if he could help us assess the impact the fire may have on neighborhood businesses and ancillary businesses that worked with Malden Mills. He agreed to make SBA councilors available for the assessment.

With my requests exhausted the Senator asked if there was anything else they could do to help. To complete the request, I asked the Senators and the Congressman to dedicate a staff person to help follow up and to coordinate federal assistance. With the cameras clicking they all agreed to the request. Yes, "Prior Proper Planning" does "Prevents Piss Poor Performance!"

With the decision made by Feuerstein to rebuild and the relief plans being implemented it was time to focus on what was next. The decision to rebuild a mature manufacturing concern generated significant interest from labor unions and economic development officials. It also drew the attention of Cardinal Law from the Archdiocese of Boston. When his office called me to express his interest it surprised me. I was unaware of the Cardinal's interest in manufacturing, but thought immediately that it was an opportunity to bring more attention to the redevelopment and the potential positive spin offs from the effort. I arranged for the Cardinal to address the community and the news media at Saint Monica's Church down the street from Malden Mills.

The Cardinal was eloquent and led the group in a prayer for those injured and for our relief efforts to be successful. He touted the benefits of good paying manufacturing jobs and offered to make the archdiocese a partner in creating new manufacturing jobs. Congressman Meehan expressed interest in the Cardinal's offer and recommended we work with him to define this partnership. I thought it was a great idea and arranged for a meeting at the Cardinal's residence in Boston with myself, Meehan, O'Neill and Feuerstein. The outcome was a plan to create a non-profit community development corporation (CDC) to help manufacturing businesses in the Arlington Mills Complex and to create workers housing in the Arlington Neighborhoods in Lawrence and Methuen. Ultimately the plan to create a CDC won a John F. Kennedy Jr. Foundation Grant and helped create momentum toward the redevelopment of the neighborhood.

Our efforts to deal with this crisis gained us Congressional recognition. On Monday, December 18, 1995, Congressman Martin Meehan entered into the Congressional Record the following citation:

"Mr. Speaker, I would like to congratulate the firemen and the emergency services workers who worked so hard to extinguish a fire which burned down the Malden Mill in Methuen Massachusetts, the region's largest textile manufacturer. I would particularly like to thank Chief Ken Bourassa of the Methuen Fire Department, who coordinated the firefighting efforts, and also Mayor Dennis DiZoglio, who is working with federal and state agencies in order to rebuild the mills which are so important to his town...

Malden Mills is the region's largest manufacturer of textiles and also the town's largest employer. Each year, the company sales exceed $500M, and the plant employs over 2,400 workers. Its presence in the region has brought economic prosperity to Methuen and contributes to Merrimack Valley's commercial growth.

Under Mayor DiZoglio's leadership plans are under way to rebuild the mills. He has secured funding from the Department of Labor and the Department of Housing and Urban Development to aid in the redevelopment. He has also been working to secure federal disaster relief funds.

I applaud the efforts of these officials to rebuild Malden Mills. With the leadership of Methuen's officials and with assistance from state and federal agencies, Malden Mills will be rebuilt quickly. Then like the Phoenix, it will rise from its ashes and once again take its place as the leading manufacturer in this region."

Building a new manufacturing building has many challenges and demands and after all the hoopla, is a business deal. This became apparent very early on in the rebuilding process. Locally Feuerstein had always been known as a shrewd businessman. In the early 90's Feuerstein had a very public battle with the city over proposed water and sewer rates. Malden Mills is the largest user of water and sewer in the city and costs are obviously a concern. Because of the significant impact these costs had on one of the largest employers in the city, Feuerstein was successful in getting the city to reduce water and sewer rate.

Cost savings were still a concern when Malden Mills began its rebuilding process. While I sincerely appreciated Feuerstein's decision to rebuild and save the jobs and the neighborhood it was certainly a business deal for the city as well. Feuerstein proposed to build a 300,000 square foot modern manufacturing building, with computerized equipment to continue manufacturing Polartec fabric. The new building would be nearly twice as large as the buildings destroyed by the fire. Malden Mills had building and business interruption insurance, which were going to defray a great deal of the cost to rebuild. In addition, it had significant good will because of their decision to rebuild and pay its workers until the plant was rebuilt, which translated into additional contracts for Polartec fabric.

The first cost issue to deal with was the building permit fees. Based on estimated construction values the building permit fees approached $300,000. The request was to waive the building permit fee. First this would be a bad precedent for the city to waive building permit fees. Once a waiver is granted others would certainly request one as well. The flood gates would be open for for-profit and not-for-profit projects to make the case that their impact would be positive for the community and justify a waiver of fees. Additionally, fees are issued to defray the cost of ensuring building codes are met and for inspections. Without fees the city would not have funds to provide proper oversight.

Clearly there would be pressure to complete construction as soon as possible to get Malden Mills operational. To resolve the permit fees, I proposed that the fees not be waived but the city would use the fees to hire an additional inspector who would be dedicated to the construction project to ensure timely inspections. Malden Mills liked the idea that there would be no delays in providing oversight and agreed to pay the fees in exchange for full access to the inspector on their timeframes.

The next cost issues dealt with property taxes and water and sewer rates. Malden Mills was paying $110,000 a year in property taxes on their old mill property and wanted to pay the same tax despite that fact that they were constructing a new building with new equipment. The new building would be significantly larger than the old buildings and had a project cost of $128,000,000, two key elements in property tax assessment. Considering the circumstances, I was willing to negotiate a tax break, but felt the offer was not fair to the community. Every year the cost to provide services to the citizens of Methuen increases due to labor negotiations, employee benefits, utilities, debt service and other needs. To cap and limit the growth in taxes did not take this into consideration so I declined the offer made by Malden Mills' attorneys.

The next day I received a call from Feuerstein's office with a request to meet to discuss the issue. When I arrived at Malden Mills corporate offices I was directed to his office. After thanking me for coming he immediately said he was not going to pay any additional taxes on the new building. He informed me he had negotiated a no new taxes deal with

Lawrence and he wanted the same deal in Methuen. The buildings were predominately in Methuen but 13% of the buildings were in Lawrence. The new building would have a similar percentage.

I reiterated my interest in doing a tax deal, but also informed him of my reasoning for rejecting the original offer. We were sitting at a table in front of his desk and he walked over to his desk picked up a set of site plans for the new building threw them on the table and said, "then I will move the building to be in Lawrence." As he made that threat I could hear the pylons for the new building being driven into the ground. While anything is possible the threat did not seem real and I told him if he needed to move the building then he should.

He then excused himself from the meeting and said he would return in a few minutes. Once he left two associates came into the office and ensured me that Feuerstein was serious and that he would move the building to Lawrence. We continued to discuss my concerns and they left the meeting once they felt there was no movement. Feuerstein then came back in the office and said, "If there is no tax deal then I will buy my water and sewer from Lawrence." Such a move would have a significant impact on water and sewer rate in Methuen since Malden Mills was the largest user of these services and consumed almost $2M a year. We both knew that was a big issue for me and one I could not let happen. But I also knew that Methuen had sufficient infrastructure to provide him with the kind of volumes Malden Mills needed and Lawrence would have to construct additional capacity to meet their needs.

Just as he had done previously, Feuerstein excused himself from the meeting and his two associates returned with the same message, Feuerstein was serious, and he would buy his water and sewer from Lawrence. We discussed the infrastructure limitations and I conceded that Lawrence could easily obtain a grant from the state or federal governments to increase capacity. But I also felt that there was so much pressure to get the mill up and running again as soon as possible that such an infrastructure project that had not been designed and competitively bid at that point would take too long. They again left, and Feuerstein returned, and we concluded our discussion without any resolution. To be honest, this tag team negotiation technique and the back and forth made me feel a little like a minor league player trying to compete with major leaguers.

Coincidently the next day Feuerstein was being recognized for his decision to stay and rebuild the mill by the Merrimack Valley Chamber of Commerce and there was a ceremony with many dignitaries being held. I obviously was invited and when I arrived, Alan Kraunallis a Methuen resident and a friend and Malden Mills' Human Resources Manager greeted me and asked me to sit next to Feuerstein on the stage.

As I sat down the ceremony began and a parade of speakers began extolling Feuerstein. Feuerstein leaned over to me and said, "Are you still mad at me?" I told him, "No I am not mad at you. You are doing what you need to do for your company, and I am doing what I need to do for my city. We just have a different perspective on how we accomplish that." He then asked to meet again and as the speakers continued to talk in front of us we took out our calendars and made an appointment to continue our negotiations.

We completed our negotiations and agreed that Malden Mills would pay $325,000 a year in taxes for the next 20 years and the industrial water and sewer rates would not increase greater than residential water and sewer rates for the term of the agreement. The new plant was also projected to be more efficient and the amount of water and sewer demand would be less. Malden Mills proposed including a co-generation plant to generate electricity and produce steam for the manufacturing process. To help the city deal with the loss of water and sewer revenue Malden Mills agreed to provide energy at a reduced rate to the city. At the end the city saw an increase in taxes and a guarantee that Malden Mills would continue to buy water and sewer from Methuen and create 800 new jobs over the next twenty years. Malden Mills received reasonable level tax payments and water and sewer rates, which gave them predictability.

Once the business deal was complete it was time to strengthen the city's fire department and improve the city's ability to rebuild from this crisis. Fighting the fire was costly. The personnel cost on the budget and the impact the fire had on our fire equipment was devastating. During the fire the ladder truck chair mechanism broke and the truck needed to be replaced. In addition, one of the older pumpers in our fleet was limited and impacted our ability to fight the fire. We also needed to prepare for rebuilding Malden Mills. The new building was going to be larger and suitable infrastructure was needed. Senator Jajuga and Senator O'Brien who help devise the response plan offered to help obtain state assistance to address these issues.

The Senators approached the legislature for a relief package to provide funds to the city to replenish our budget and replace our damaged and outdated equipment. They also sought funds to support the needed infrastructure. They wanted to brief the chairman of the Senate Ways and Means Committee and invited him to tour the site and meet with officials from Methuen and Lawrence to get a good handle on the needs. While Methuen was the lead in fighting the fire, and overseeing the rebuilding of Malden Mills both cities were impacted, and both were offered an opportunity to outline their needs.

This was a golden opportunity to make the city whole so I asked the city auditor to prepare a budget impact analysis to share with the chairman. I also asked the fire chief to describe how the fire equipment was damaged and limited. In addition, I asked the DPW director to describe the water and sewer needs to support the rebuilding and the current capacity deficiencies that needed to be corrected. He described the size of the pipes and the length of pipes that needed to be replaced. We also wanted to improve the streets and sidewalks leading to the new building and the director prepared an overview of the plans with measurements of sidewalks and streets proposed for repair along with the number of historic lights that could be installed to complement the Malden Mills investment.

Senator Jajuga asked me to introduce the department heads and present our needs. I thanked the senators for arranging this briefing and thanked the chairman for coming. The department heads were articulate and thorough. Once they completed their presentations Senator O'Brien asked the Lawrence representative to present their needs. The Lawrence representative stood up and said, "We would like the same as Methuen" and sat back down. The senator was clearly embarrassed and offered to provide more specific information about Lawrence's need in the forthcoming weeks. In the end the legislature approved a relief package for both communities and we had sufficient funds to repair our budget, upgrade our fire department and prepare for the redevelopment of Malden Mills.

Leaders are not born they are made. They are made when they face a crisis and need to solve problems with hard work, good management skills and a purpose.

Chapter 5

"I Don't Know What He Is Talking About But I'm Opposed"

Public officials are constantly reminded that they work for the people. In order to properly work for the people, you need to know what they are thinking. The mechanism most often used to form an opinion on what people are thinking is through civic engagement. However, civic engagement is not as easy as calling a meeting and listening to the people. Many people are intimidated by government and are mistrustful. They don't understand how the process works and come to meetings full of mistrust and try to use threats and intimidation as opposed to providing meaningful engagement. In a democracy public participation is the foundation on which decisions are made. You need to take into consideration the feelings of those people who are impacted by decisions or who are interested in the decisions that are being made. This interactive process is where the challenge begins.

People mistrust the government because it will not do what they want it to do. They come to a meeting angry and provide very little useful opinions except verifying opposition. For example, land use permitting requires that the public has an opportunity to express their opinions and concerns regarding pending developments. While community development director for the City of Peabody, I helped create and develop the Centennial Industrial Park. The industrial park became one of the premier parks in northeastern Massachusetts. We were able to obtain funding to construct an interchange off I 95 to provide good access, constructed a rail spur for freight use, and obtained an EDA grant to construct the necessary infrastructure to support the industrial development. The city owned the land and when each parcel was sold to an industrial concern the city through the Peabody Development Authority would include in the land disposition agreement building standards that the company would have to follow. The land disposition agreement ensured that a building was constructed with suitable masonry products, appropriate landscaping and high design features. The intent was to maximize job creation and tax revenue by requiring class A or B buildings and uses as opposed to warehousing and other low-end concerns.

Centennial was reaching capacity and the mayor wanted to continue encouraging industrial development on land industrially zones adjacent to Centennial but for the most part privately owned. Since we did not have control of the land we needed to find another way to ensure that the building design standards key to the success of Centennial would be in place for future development. We came up with an idea to create an overlay zoning district on the adjacent land that would require set design standard. The overlay district would be called the Designated Development District (DDD) and site plan review would be required to ensure the standards were met. Today this approach is called form base code zoning (16) and has gained popularity but at the time this was a new approach.

In Massachusetts zoning changes require a public hearing before the planning board and then before the city council. We scheduled a public hearing before the planning board to gain feedback on the idea. Another responsibility of the planning board is to consider land subdivision requests. Owners of land can build a roadway and infrastructure to support a housing development subject to zoning and approval by the planning board and the board must hold a public hearing on the request. Peabody is a desirable community to live in and developers are always looking for new development opportunities to meet the market demands. New housing means changes in existing neighborhoods and folks don't like change. Opposition to new housing is common and people attend public meetings to register their opposition to new subdivisions.

The night we had scheduled the hearing for the overlay there were two other public hearings scheduled to consider two new subdivisions. Our public hearing was sandwiched between the two other hearings. As anticipated the attendees were opposed to the new subdivision and forcibly spoke in opposition at the first hearing. Usually the last people who move to a neighborhood are the first to oppose any new development. This was somewhat the case that night and many of the attendees were unfamiliar with Centennial Park since they were new to the community. Planning boards very rarely make a decision after a hearing and wait for feedback from city department heads on the impact of a subdivision before making a decision and the attendees were also unfamiliar with this process and remained to hear a decision.

When we began our public hearing, the Chairman asked if there was anyone who wanted to speak in favor of the overlay. We had prepared a complete presentation for the public hearing and presented it at that time. We had taken pictures of buildings we were trying to prevent through the zoning overlay and showed pictures of what we wanted to encourage. We talked about the development of Centennial and the intent of the overlay to ensure good development with good jobs and new tax revenue. The Chairman then asked if there was anyone else that would like to speak in favor, with none, he asked the other board members if they had any questions, they had none. The Chairman then asked if anyone opposed the overlay. A person who attended the first public hearing came to the podium and said, "I don't know what he is talking about but I'm opposed." With that the crowd erupted in applause and cheers. Another person who was waiting for the next hearing on the other subdivision went to the podium and said, "I agree with this gentleman I'm opposed."

The Chairman then closed the public hearing. At the public hearing before the city council no one spoke in opposition to the overlay and it was approved by the planning board and ultimately the city council.

Mistrust even enters into a discussion when you ask peoples' opinion if you should consider something. When I was Mayor of Methuen, I was approached by a developer who had identified some land adjacent to Route 110 and a short distance from I 495 that could potentially be developed into an office/R&D industrial site. This developer had a good reputation and had developed a similar development in the neighboring community of Andover. These are good developments in that they are high-end for tax purposes and create good paying jobs and require very little municipal services.

The land under consideration was behind a series of single family dead-end streets. The streets were developed before the extension of sewer and water to the area and did not have municipal sewer. Septic systems were constantly failing, and the neighborhoods were constantly requesting sewer be extended. Funds were not available to extend the service and the neighborhoods were not in full favor of betterment assessments to gain sewer.

The land would need to be rezoned for the proposed use. I thought in exchange for the zoning the developer would be required to extend water and sewer to each street when extending it for the development and that the developer would pave each street, which in effect would give everyone a new neighborhood. We could also preclude any access to the development from their streets and require the developer to acquire the last street with only 3 homes and use that as their access to the site and do any traffic improvements warranted.

The developer agreed, and I offered to reach out to the neighbors and invite them to a Saturday morning meeting at city hall to present the idea. Obviously, this was before any permitting or hearings associated with zoning would begin, just a meeting to take the neighbors "temperature" as to their interest in pursuing the idea. Since the neighbors may not be familiar with the kind of development being proposed I suggested the developer do a rendering.

The meeting was well attended and the two east end councilors where there to hear if the neighbors would be interested in the idea. I explained the idea to the group and then asked, "what do you think?"

The first comments were very negative. "Are you trying to jam this development down our throats?" I assured them that that was not the case and I was only floating the idea to get their reaction. The negativity continued and one person said, "If this is only an idea then why do you have a rendering of what the buildings would look like?"

I walked over to the easel that held the rendering and threw it across the room. I then told them that if they did not want the development then it is gone just like the rendering. The rendering was only there to show them that this was not going to be a smoke stack kind of industrial development. If the majority of the neighbors did not want to pursue the idea we would stop our discussions with the developer. I then called for a show of hands in favor of continuing the discussion with the developer. While there were a number who wanted to continue the discussion, it was clear that the majority did not and I told them the idea was off the table. Some pleaded with their neighbors to keep an open mind because of the significant improvements being offered but since the mistrust had set in I ended our discussion with the offer to reconsider only if a majority came in and requested reconsideration. The neighbors never came back.

Sometimes mistrust is not just about a government action but the institution itself. As the Deputy General Manager for Planning and Development at the MBTA, I was responsible for deciding where the MBTA should invest its limited capital dollars to expand service. We would regularly analyze the feasibility of a project and attempt to gauge the benefits of the project to determine the most worthy projects to advance. One such project was restoration of Green Line service in the Jamaica Plain neighborhood of Boston. The MBTA had discontinued service to upgrade E line tracks leading to the neighborhood and decided not to upgrade tracks in Jamaica Plain due to poor service caused by narrow streets and auto congestion. The potential to restore service needed to be analyzed and public meetings to solicit comments on the findings needed to be held.

An initial public meeting was held to help the MBTA decide on parameters of the study and decide on the elements of concerns to focus on and the criteria it should use to evaluate these concerns during the study. One of the tactics used to get meaningful feedback from the public is attempting to relate to the people in attendance. You want those in attendance to have confidence in the process that the people conducting the meeting are not a bureaucratic enemy, but people just like them.

Before a meeting started I would mingle with those in attendance and try to strike up a conversation about where they lived, about their family and also interject information about my family in hopes of relating to the person. At this meeting I used the same technique and while talking to one neighbor she said "I know what you are doing. I don't want to hear about your family. I have hated the MBTA for thirty years, so I hate you!" The mistrust was institutional as it seemed to be most of the time at the MBTA and we received very little productive feedback on the parameters for the study.

The mistrust sometimes turns into threats. Another MBTA analysis I was in charge of conducting was to assess the impacts the proposed extension of the blue line to the North Shore would have on selected cities. Because it was so hard to get meaningful feedback we would try various methods to encourage a dialogue with those in attendance at public meetings. At a meeting in Salem Massachusetts, we attempted to break the crowd up into smaller groups to discuss potential impacts like noise, air quality, traffic etc. When I announced the format of the meeting many of the attendees protested. They wanted a tradition public hearing format where they could speak at a podium and express their support or opposition to the extension.

I told them that a series of public hearing would be held once the analysis was concluded to gain feedback on the findings as well as support or opposition to the project. I asked them to give this format a try so we could hear directly from them any concerns in those areas we were studying. As we began using the new format people continued to protest and threatened that if a traditional public hearing was not held they would complain to their senators and representatives and demand we come out again and hold one. This was not an idle threat and I knew the politicians would demand we go back again so I ceased the discussions underway at the various tables and reconvened the entire group and held a public hearing.

One by one, speakers said the same thing for an hour and a half, they were opposed to the extension. After we closed the meeting I asked one speaker if she thought the meeting was productive and she said "Yes, I wanted everyone who came tonight to hear what I had to say. In the other format you would have been the only one to hear what I had to say." We never received any advice on the impacts of the extension and the pubic had two meetings at the conclusion of the study to voice their opposition to the extension.

One threat that never goes away is the threat not to vote for you. During the debate to privatize the trash pickup in Methuen a citizen approached me and said "My daughter is a CPA she has looked at the budget and said this will not save the city any money. I voted for you and if you do this I will not vote for you again." I told him that calculating the savings was not an easy task and that the line items for trash pickup and disposal did not show the true savings available to the city. I then put my hand on his shoulder and said, "I appreciate the fact that you voted for me the first time, but I need to do what I think is best and if you cannot vote for me again I understand." I then concluded by saying "I had a life before I was mayor and I will have one after I am mayor."

Knowing that a politician's future depends on getting reelected people try to intimidate you to change your position. During my first year in office as mayor I was invited to be the quest on a local radio talk show. During the show a woman caller asked if I was responsible for enforcing local ordinances. I responded in the affirmative and she then asked if I would be enforcing the zoning ordinance to prevent businesses from operating out of a residence. I told her I was unaware of any violations and she then announced that Councilor Joe Pappalardo was running a business out of his home and wanted to know if I would enforce the ordinance or continue to let him do so because he was a councilor.

Since Pappalardo was one of my first supporters I knew I had been ambushed. I told her I would look into the allegation and moved on to the next caller. Pappalardo was a landscaper and ran his business out of his home. Because elected officials are in positions to make decisions they make enemies. The caller was an "enemy" and wanted to use the system to hurt him. When I looked at the complaint I found that Pappalardo did indeed run a business out of his home and stored his trucks on site. His lot abutted I 495 and because of the lot configuration the trucks could not be seen from the street or very easily from abutters.

The ordinance reads that an aggrieved party can make a complaint of violation and the building inspector would enforce the ordinance. The definition of an aggrieved party is an abutter within 300 feet of the property in question. Since the caller was not an abutter and we learned she actually lived over two miles away I decided not to enforce the violation. But I told the building inspector that if an abutter did make any complaints to enforce the ordinance. Pappalardo had lived there many years even before he was a councilor and neighbors had never complained.

While I diffused the issue, and avoided the misuse of the ordinance as a weapon and a political awkward situation for me the issue did not go away. Pappalardo was concerned that if an abutter did ultimately make a complaint be would be forced to discontinue running his business out of his home. He knew of a number of other businesses that operated out of their homes who would be adversely affected and proposed a zoning referendum that would allow home businesses to be run out of residences. He proposed a referendum versus a change in the ordinance to avoid any conflict of interest. He asked for my support. While some home businesses can coexist in residential neighborhoods because of their benign operations others cannot. People move into a neighborhood to live and raise their families. Some business activities bring traffic, noise and may not be compatible with children so I told him I would not be in favor of the referendum. I told him I preferred to continue enforcing the current ordinance by only aggrieved parties.

Methuen is very much a blue collar community and there are many businesses that are operated out of homes in neighborhoods across the community and so support for the referendum was greater than I expected. There was a very active campaign supporting the referendum. A few months before the referendum vote I was asked by Pappalardo to attend a meeting in a home with supporters of the referendum. As I entered the home I was ushered downstairs to the meeting. As I got to the bottom of the stairs I could see that a long table had been set up with over 25 business owners present along with reporters from the *Eagle Tribune* and the *Methuen Journal*. Each business owner took a turn telling me how important the issue was to their business survival in hopes of changing my position. Each one also indicated that they had supported me in the last election and that they would not support me in the future unless I changed my mind. The reporters were there to add more intimidation and to record my decision. Once they completed their comments I thanked them all for inviting me and for their support in the past. I reiterated my position and again offered to enforce the ordinance by aggrieved party only and told them I had to do what I thought was best for the community and if they could not support me in the future I understood.

One bit of irony to this story is that the initial support I received from Pappalardo was significant. I gained access to supporters and momentum and may not have been able to get elected without his assistance. One of the first things he did when I ran for mayor was drive me around town to meet people he knew. We went to dozens of homes and he would start each visit by introducing me and saying, "One thing I like about Dennis is while we may not always agree I think he will do what he thinks is best for Methuen." In some ways I do feel like I betrayed his support, but I did have to do what I thought was best and do not regret my decision to oppose the referendum. The referendum was defeated 46% for and 54% against. Pappalardo did not seek reelection in 1995 and our relationship has been strained ever since.

Using a large group to intimidate an elected official is a common tactic. As mayor you need to keep your eye on the big picture despite the political fallout. One such incident took place in 1996. There were over 1,000 children enrolled in Methuen Youth Soccer. The leaders of the association raised the critical need for more soccer playing fields. Their program was severely limited and there was talk of limiting participation and reducing the number of children that could participate. A Presbyterian church in the city had indicated that they were able to raise funds and purchase a former apple orchard in the west end and in an effort to expand their congregation offered some of the land for use as soccer fields. Methuen Youth Soccer was willing to raise funds to construct three soccer fields on the land. While the land was owned by a religious institution and exempt from zoning I thought it was important to brief the neighborhood of this proposed partnership. At a public meeting the neighborhood was strongly opposed to the project. They feared traffic impacts and visitors coming to their neighborhood. We discussed buffering options and traffic control ideas, but many of the neighbors were concerned about the unknown.

After the meeting a person who had supported my reelection approached me and asked if I would be willing to meet with some of the neighbors to discuss the mitigation ideas. These "come to discuss" meetings are usually arranged by someone who knows you and you have a relationship.

They arranged for the meeting to be held in a small function facility. Sure enough the hall was at full capacity when I arrived. The thirty or so people who had showed up were not there to discuss mitigation but wanted to stop the project. "We asked you here tonight to tell you that we will never support you again if this project goes forward." I asked them to put themselves in my shoes. "I have over 1,000 Methuen kids who want to play soccer and nowhere to have them play." I continued by reminding them that we did not have money available to buy land or budgeted funds to construct the fields and that I had to find a creative way to meet this community need. I pleaded with them to work with me to make sure that the project had the smallest impact possible on the neighborhood. The site was approximately a mile from my house and I knew many of the people in the room, but I needed to keep an eye on the big picture. Since the church was exempted from zoning the soccer fields were built.

Sometimes public engagement is a "full contact sport" and trying to make it a productive experience is very difficult. The best opportunity to engage the public in a meaningful way is to approach them with a clean slate. However, it is the responsibility of public officials to bring ideas, concepts and projects to the public for input and the opportunities to ask what the public thinks without specifics are rare. This dynamic occurs most during master and long-term planning efforts. Asking citizens how they want their community to grow, or the kinds of housing needs they have, or what areas funding should be prioritized is a lot easier than asking them if an in-law apartment should be approved in their neighborhood. When it personally affects them, the public is not shy in giving their opinion; yet if it does not affect their daily life they seem apathetic. A public meeting is held on the proposed $100M annual budget, and no one attends; a ZBA variance public hearing is held, and the room is full.

Chapter 6

"You Hold This Boy's Future in Your Hands, Committee"(17)

After the election my uncle gave me a plaque for my desk that read "The Buck Stops Here". The quote is commonly associated with President Harry Truman who believed that the president has to make decisions and is responsible for those decisions. The same goes for the mayor. People hold the mayor accountable even if it may not be their decision.

During my second term in office a company obtained a permit to hold a "Rave" in vacant space at the Methuen Mall. A "Rave" is a large dance party with loud electronic music. The music is accompanied by laser light shows and can attract drug use. At the time the word "Rave" was not familiar to the police and the licensing board and did not draw any particular attention or concern. The police assigned a detail and the dance was held. The evening was a disaster. The people who attended the dance became unruly and police from surrounding communities had to be called to assist in quelling the crowd.

Many in the public were outraged that we would permit such an event and blamed me for allowing the event to be held. Although I was not involved directly in the permitting of the event the criticism was aimed at me. I was involved in dealing with the aftermath of the event like the cost to handle the problem and the development of procedures to prevent a similar occurrence, so I was ultimately responsible.

Because the mayor is going to be held responsible for what happens in the community there is a natural tendency for the mayor to want to control the decision-making process. But, government regularly establishes committees to help make decisions and controlling a committee is not an option. Yes, a mayor can try to control a committee but there are many committees and the time associated with trying to influence a committee would be too consuming. It would also require using so much "political capital" that it would limit the ability to influence other decisions. It could also create a backlash from committee members who question their role and don't want to be perceived as pawns for the mayor.

The mayor needs to create a meaningful and defined role for committees. There is a relationship that must be established that directs a committee but does not over manage their work. Before I arrived in Methuen the town council had created the Methuen Public Safety Commission. It was made up of citizens who were charged with increasing cooperation between residents and public safety officials, a laudable objective with a positive agenda. The idea of a commission actually fit in with the effort to create a community policing program in Methuen, which I was in favor of implementing. Once I came on board a number of commission members approached me about expanding their role with the idea of holding public meetings throughout the community. They were also considering asking the police department to attend the meetings and report to them on their activities. I had some concerns with this approach.

When the commission was formed they held a public meeting and the turnout was disappointing. The turnout was explained as apathy. I thought holding more public meetings would result in the same attendance and not accomplish much. In addition, if there was little public participation the commission might seek to expand their meeting to be more like tribunals where the police report to them. This was a transitional time for the police department as they were just starting to embrace community policing. Community policing is based on improved dialogue with the residents. I was concerned that the police might see this interaction with the commission as their dialogue and might not reach out to individual neighbors and neighborhoods where community policing is at its best. Neighborhood dialogue can result in crime watch efforts and crime problem solving techniques.

I thought that a stronger role for the commission would be to promote and market the efforts of the police. The commissioners could be the advocates for community policing and help residents and town officials' band together to fight crime. The chairman of the commission was also very active on the local cable television station and I thought that it would be a good vehicle for the commission to use to promote and market the police programs. When I broached the idea with the chairman he was very supportive since he was hoping for the cable station to be more involved in the community. He sold the idea to his fellow commissioners and we had a meaningful and defined role for the commission.

One of the first television shows sponsored by the commission involved telling the community about a problem-solving effort in one of the neighborhoods. A neighborhood was seeing a rise in drug activity in an adjacent park. Police working with the residents learned that the basketball court attracted young people from outside the neighborhood and drug sales increased when the court was used. The young people would stay hours playing full court basketball. As an experiment we took down one of the baskets and made the court a half-court facility. Because they wanted to play full-court basketball the use of the court plummeted and the drug problems were gone. The half-court remained only as an attraction to the local children. Community policing was off and running and the commission played a meaningful role in getting it off the ground.

Sometimes committees are less about public involvement and more about bringing expertise to a decision or advice on how to proceed. There are so many issues a mayor must deal with that it is virtually impossible to be knowledgeable about them all so help can be beneficial. I had one such case and formed a committee to help analyze and inform my decision.

Before I came into office the town made a decision to buy burial crypts for Elmwood Cemetery. The use of crypts can accommodate tandem use and can increase capacity at a cemetery. While on the surface this looks like a sound business decision, in Methuen it was not. McLaughlin the

Town Manager asked the council to approve the purchase of 240 crypts without the benefit of a procurement process. It was explained that the purchase of crypts did not require the traditional procurement procedure and that the price was advantageous because of a sales opportunity. The town manager had the crypts delivered to take advantage of this sale before the council had voted approval. In addition to the lack of a traditional procurement process the council had to enact an emergency preamble to pay for the crypts in a timely manner since they were already delivered. As you can imagine this decision along with the unusual business practices drew attention from the public and became quite controversial. When I came into office I had to deal with a prolonged cemetery trust fund deficit since the sale of the crypts were on an as needed basis.

While we needed to deal with the fund shortfall we also needed to address burial capacity issues at the cemetery since once the crypts were all sold Elmwood plot expansion was limited. I was approached about the possibility to meet this future need with the construction of a mausoleum. A mausoleum is a structure/building which allows for multi tandem above ground burials with the use of very little land. There was no immediate need because there was capacity with the unsold crypts but eventually there would be a need for more burial spots and this might be a way to increase capacity without buying more land. I was hesitant to make a decision because of all the previous controversy and the uncertainty of when the need would warrant action.

I wanted knowledgeable people about burial and future needs. I appointed the three most prominent mortuary owners and the chairman of the council of aging to an ad hoc committee and asked them to meet with the mausoleum developer, analyze the need and assess the business plan. Creating a committee gave the process some transparency and objectivity. They met with the developer, checked his references and assessed expansion potential. They recommended not to precede with the developer due to negative reference checks and recommended land acquisition for expansion purposes. With their advice we abandoned the mausoleum idea and offered crypt sales on a pre-need basis which was not allowed in the past and used the proceeds from the sales to buy some abutting property for future expansion.

Up to this point the committees referenced are discretionary or ad hoc but most committees in a community are standing committees. Committees such as planning boards, zoning boards of appeal, conservation commissions, boards of health and historic district commissions, have a significant influence on public policy. These committees make decision that affect how a community grows, how a community creates affordable housing, and how a community protects the environment or its historic character.

It is unethical to micro manage these permit issuing committees. The roles of these committees are defined by ordinance or state statute so there is very little the mayor can or should do to influence decisions. Staff recommendation can help but they are free to make an independent decision.

As the appointing authority you can try to ensure that the members are as objective as possible. For the most part members are appointed after they file a talent bank application. Applications usually give a prospective member an opportunity to identify a committee that interests them and provides some information on their background. While helpful it does not always give you a feel if the applicant will be objective and call "balls and strikes".

I tried to meet each person individually and hear from them what motivated them about serving their community. People who indicated any bias, positive or negative about previous committee decisions, or individuals in the community, or complaints about strict or liberal interpretation of statues or ordinances were not appointed. You want them to be objective, but you don't want them to be too rigid or too liberal in their decision making. Each case requires an objective review. The world is not always black or white, there is a lot of grey and committee members have to use their best judgment in making a decision.

Appointing the best candidates possible can help strengthen decisions and reduce challenges to the process. Many people go to the council when they want to issue a complaint. For example, a developer complained to the council under public participation that the conservation commission was being arbitrary in the decision to deny him an order of conditions and they lacked the qualifications to make that determination.

During a mayor's report the council asked me to respond to the complaint. I told them while unfamiliar with the decision, the commission members where well qualified and I was confident that their decision was not arbitrary or capricious. I offered to have the commission members attend one of their meetings and discuss their qualifications and their approach when considering a decision. I cautioned the council that this would not be an inquisition and that the specifics of the case in question could not be reviewed or overturned but perhaps the council would feel as confident as I that the decision was appropriate after the discussion.

The night of the meeting a long table was brought into the Great Hall for the commissioners to sit and talk with the council. I started the meeting by commending the commissioners' work and asked if they would go around the table and tell the councilors their background. One by one they talked about their qualifications. The council heard that one member had an environmental degree, one member was an attorney, one member was a businessman with a MBA and one member had an engineering degree. The council quickly learned that the members where well qualified citizens trying to help the community make informed decisions. Once they heard how the professional staff helped the commissioners make these informed decisions the council began complimenting the commissioners and expressed support for their work. The complaint went no further.

Not all committee decisions go the way you hope them to go. While you hope the pre-appointment interview process brings some objectivity to the decision making there are no guarantees. Decisions coming out of these standing committees need to be monitored, particularly when appointments are up and reappointments are pending.

One such decision involved the efforts to revitalize the downtown of Methuen. The city had acquired through back taxes a derelict building in the downtown. The city wanted to tear down the building and create additional parking to support downtown businesses. The building was located adjacent to the Spicket River, which runs through the downtown and required an order of conditions from the conservation commission to manage the demolition. A former member of the conservation commission and city council member who ran a towing business had hoped to persuade the city to sell him the building for storage of vehicles. The proposed use was inconsistent with the city plans. The former member approached the chairman of the commission and influenced him to delay issuing the order of conditions to give him more time to convince the city to sell him the building. Confronted with the pending reappointment of the chairman I sent a letter thanking him for his years of service to the community and advised him that I wanted to give others an opportunity to serve their community and he was not reappointed.

Chapter 7

"If You Are Not Part Of The Solution You're Part Of The Problem"

In the 1976 Academy Award winning movie "*Network*", fictional newscaster Howard Beale tells his viewers to get up out of their chairs, go to their window, open it and shout out for all to hear "I'm as mad as hell and I'm not going to take it anymore!"

Sometimes when citizens get mad as hell they don't go to the window but decide to run for political office. They run because the government did something they didn't like or the government didn't do something they wanted. Their intent in running is to make a difference, but they make very little impact on changing the system they came to fix if they are elected.

The reason they are not effective is that when they become mad they blame those already in power for the problems they see. They criticize those public officials and sometimes even insult them when complaining. They do not have a positive relationship with these public officials and when they get elected have virtually no working relationship with them that they can use to change public policy. They do not know how to formulate public policy to change the system or possess the skill set to build consensus even if they can identify ways to change the system. Because they are ineffective they tend to focus on constituent services. They can have some successes making the system responsive to constituent issues and can stay in power because of this role. They actually feel comfortable in this role because they are advocating for people they feel have been let down by government and continue to be mad as hell.

Chuck Turner was a long-time activist in the City of Boston. He was a champion for workers and led efforts to establish worker collaboratives. Upset with a lack of support for workers and African Americans, Turner ran for Boston City Council in 1999 and was elected by a 693 vote margin. It was described that Turner had a volatile relationship with his fellow councilors. He made derogatory statements about fellow councilors and accused them of "institutional racism." He served on the council until 2010 when he was expelled by his fellow councilors by an 11-1 vote due to a corruption conviction. (18)

During his 10 years in office Turner had little success working with the council. He was able to secure only two legislative successes. The first was a resolution honoring Martin Luther King and the second, and notable, he authored an ordinance protecting transgender persons from discrimination. Outside of complaining he had very little success changing the system he came to fix.

Dorothy Kalil a long-time resident in Methuen was a staunch opponent of cluster home development. Communities that have cluster housing allow land developers to build homes on lots that are smaller than required by zoning provided the that the number of lots allowed is consistent with the number of lots allowed by zoning and that the land not used by the homes be made permanent and protected open space. She was a strong supporter of two-acre zoning and wanted to see Methuen be prominently a community of single family homes sited on two acre lots. She was angry that the council was considering cluster zoning and supporters of her anti-growth approach encouraged her to run for council.

While she lost her second run for council in 1985 her opponent passed away in office, so she was made the councilor from the west end to complete his term. When she ran to stay on the council in 1987 she was initially disappointed again as she appeared to lose the election by just seven votes. When questioned by the press regarding her loss she attacked her opponent as being in the pocket of developers and announced that she would not attend any more council meetings, stating "I refuse to tie up my time for people who refused to come and vote for me". After eleven absentee ballots were added to the election totals the election was a dead heat. After a recount it stood as a dead heat and a special election was called for on January 12th to break the tie. The comments Kalil made greatly affected her election bid and she was defeated by 166 votes. (19)

She continued to complain about the electorate "I never let these people down and I feel they let me down". After her defeat she swore off politics "I don't like politics and will not run again."

She continued her crusade against cluster zoning and in 2010 she did run for office again and was elected to the Charter Review Commission. The council placed the creation of the charter commission on the ballot to gauge support for a review of the charter and if approved would elect nine citizens to serve on the commission. The nine candidates with the most votes were elected to the commission. I also ran for the commission fearing that the rhetoric from some of the thirty or so candidates suggested they wanted to change the way government worked in Methuen to be more of a town form, which I opposed. It would be very difficult to manage a community the size of Methuen through small town governing mechanisms. I placed first and Kalil placed ninth.

From the very beginning Kalil was abrasive at the commission meetings. She advocated for those positions she was strongly in favor off and made little effort to build consensus around her positions. When she made suggestions, she was sarcastic during her presentations. Kalil had also been the woman who called me on the talk show that generated the home business referendum. Joe Pappalardo was also elected to the Commission and they clashed immediately after the meetings began as well. Only her suggestion to modify the number of signatures needed for citizen petitions made it into the final recommendations.

Councilor Maureen Donovan was re-elected councilor-at-large in 1993 at the same time I was elected mayor. Her notoriety came when she championed improvements to a "five corners" intersection in Methuen. The Streets of Pelham, Lowell, Railroad and Osgood come together and created a number of conflicts which resulted in many car accidents. The improvement project was significant and qualified for federal funding. Projects funded through federal funding take longer to develop. Funds need to be programmed, designs need to be completed and the projects need to be publicly bid.

Donovan worked at the senior citizen center on Lowell Street, less than a quarter of a mile from the intersection. Many seniors would complain about the unsafe condition at the intersection and Donovan became upset that the project was languishing through the bureaucratic process. She organized a protest and coordinated picketing at the intersection and at town hall blaming the council for the delays. Shortly after her protests the project started to move forward. As you can imagine many citizens told Donovan she should run for council because of her success.

In 1993 she was the top vote getter for the at-large council seats. Over the course of her eight years in office Donovan submitted only one ordinance for consideration. Coincidently it was one I suggested she consider filing on behalf of a constituent, a pooper scooper ordinance for parks and playgrounds. Donovan's primary focus was on constituent services. She felt comfortable fighting for citizen requests. Donovan and I had a good relationship during the first four years we served together. However, over the last two years she became frustrated with what she believed was her inability to change the system that motivated her to run in the first place. She began to use her vote to force change. She voted against awarding a contract to construct historic displays at the local historic museum, the Tenney Gatehouse. The contract was being funded with grant funds, but she preferred the funds go to subsidize the installation of sewer in a neighborhood. She also voted to cut a department head position from the budget as a punitive measure for approval of a project she opposed.

Advocates come to power because they believe the system is broken, but they have no idea on how to bring about change. Their approach to governing is combative and not constructive and they are not able to solve the problems they came to fix. They only add to the problem government has in making decisions; they add to the gridlock; they add to its negative perception; and they are clearly not part of the solution.

Chapter 8

"Who, What, When, Where, Why & How"

When you attend journalism school you are taught that the responsibility of the press is to report on events, stating who, what, when, where, why and how-and when it comes to government hold it accountable to the people. Many times, telling the story can help government officials advance their objectives but all too often the press can be seen as the enemy. The press can be a natural ally to the government by getting the news out but it can also hurt the government by interfering with its operations, questioning its motives, and challenging public officials' credibility. The press and government officials have a different definition of how to hold government officials and institutions accountable to the public and it shows when they interact.

From a government officials' perspective, the press is at its best when it can let people know what is happening in a community. When I worked in Taunton Massachusetts, the City was working diligently to develop the Miles Standish Industrial Park. One of the efforts included applying to be the site of the Massachusetts Technology Center, a public/private partnership with the tech community to construct a research and development center to help promote technology in the state. The competition was keen and the city failed to get the designation. The city's application got the attention of the *Taunton Gazette* and the *Boston Globe*. The *Boston Globe Magazine* featured the city's failed application but highlighted that the attention had resulted in private companies discovering and locating facilities in the Miles Standish Industrial Park. In the article I was quoted saying, "We may have lost the battle to get the tech center located in Taunton, but we won the war and are now seeing the benefits." The article brought even more attention to the city's efforts and Miles Standish Industrial Park is now one of the premier industrial parks in Massachusetts.

When the bad reputation of a neighborhood stifles private investment, a series of well-placed articles highlighting efforts and the resulting successes can change that perspective and help revitalize a neighborhood. When I worked in Lawrence, we began buying vacant boarded up homes, rehabilitating them, and selling them to first time homeowners. The human-interest stories published in the *Eagle Tribune* followed those efforts and generated new interest in the neighborhood and a Laundromat and plating company soon opened in the neighborhood.

News stories can help encourage citizens to participate in government efforts. To build community pride we established the "Methuen on the Move" campaign, a multi-faceted campaign that included community clean-ups, the adoption of traffic islands and plant flowers, and community events. Positive articles in the *Methuen Journal* and the *Eagle Tribune* helped attract many citizens to participate in these programs.

Getting the press to cover these positive stories is not always easy. At the end of the day newspapers and media outlets are businesses that need to generate revenue by selling advertisement. When advertisers decide where to put their advertising dollars they look for those outlets that give them the biggest bang for their buck. News outlets need to show they are the best place to put those limited dollars so they need to show they can attract more viewers than the others. This competition affects how they interact with government officials.

When I worked in Peabody the city was served by four daily newspapers; *Peabody Times, Salem News, Lynn Item, Beverly Times,* and three weekly journals. When the mayor wanted to get specific stories out into the community he would hold a press conference and release the information together to all the outlets. Reporters would ask questions and there would be somewhat of a dialogue in framing the stories. It was a fair way of releasing the information and it helped frame an accurate picture of the story. When I was elected Mayor of Methuen I called my first press conference and the *Eagle Tribune* declined to attend. The response was "we don't go to press conferences". The competition between the *Methuen Journal*, a weekly, and the *Tribune* was fierce and neither one wanted to see a level playing field and they decided the best way to stay ahead of the other was to try to out scoop each other. Of course, to out scoop the other they needed to search for stories. They were constantly interviewing public officials searching for that story and interfering with the daily work of these officials.

This type of interference was severe during the Malden Mills fire. The sheer size of the event and the local, regional and even national implications of the story attracted dozens of news outlets. Television, newspapers, radio and internet outlets flooded the city and actually interfered with the city's response to the fire. Each outlet wanted to get the scoop and an exclusive interview or comment from a public official engaged in the response. This interference started at the very beginning of the fire. When news got out that the fire was blazing news outlets began calling the dispatch center at the fire station to get details and comments from city officials. The volume was so great that two extra firefighters had to be called in to supplement the work of the firefighter on duty. The ability of the dispatchers to coordinate mutual aid and other public safety personnel was compromised.

This interference became overwhelming and chaotic as the news outlets wanted to interview frontline personnel. They demanded an interview with the fire chief as he tried to focus on the problems at hand. They wanted to sit down with myself and other elected officials while we tried to prepare for an effective response. The building inspector could not leave the site without reporting to them what he found. It got so bad I had to stop all interviews with the news media and had to schedule regular press briefings where all the public officials engaged in the response were made available to address the press questions. Although there was a virtual quarantine over press interviews the press continued to hound all the officials for an exclusive.

As the intensity of the event subsided the interest from the press diminished significantly and five days after the fire only one news outlet attend the scheduled briefing. Reporters were so motivated to get the story that they became abrasive and demanding when requesting interviews. They even became sarcastic when they got what they requested. *CNN* had been asking for an interview with me regarding how older mill towns still relied on traditional industries like Malden Mills and what communities did to retain those types of companies. It was obviously a background piece and I put off the request until things calmed down. Once the interview was set and the cameras were set up I mentioned to the crew that my father regularly watched *CNN* and he lived in Florida and he would get a chance to see his son on television. The camera man looked at me and said, "Yea sure that is your only motivation to be on our show".

The need to sell advertising should not be underestimated. The headlines and the stories are there to sell newspapers, so advertisers will advertise. When we were able to attract a developer to purchase the tired Methuen Mall and construct a million square feet of commercial space with five restaurants and a twenty-screen movie theater I scheduled a briefing with the editor of the *Eagle Tribune*. Once I presented the plan he interrupted me and said the publisher would want to see this plan. While I had not met the publisher before and would not expect to meet with him on a regular basis his presence there told me he saw advertising dollars and it was significant for his business.

Outside of beating the competition to a story what also sells newspapers is exposing a "Gotcha" moment. A headline that highlights an elected official's faux par or even a perceived faux par sells newspapers. I learned about this "Gotcha" moment innocently. When in Peabody, a reporter from the *Peabody Times* called me looking for a story. She was under a deadline and had nothing to report. She begged me for a story and I told her that the mayor was forming a committee to promote affordable housing in the community. The Mass Housing Partnership, a statewide organization, was advocating that communities establish an affordable housing committee to provide feedback on housing programs and suggest ways communities could encourage affordable housing. I described the purpose of the committee and gave her the names of the people the mayor was appointing. The next day I picked up the newspaper and the headlines read "Mayor Appoints Supporters to Housing Committee". The article suggested that the mayor had appointed his political supporters to the committee to control its work. This ad hoc committee had no regulatory responsibilities. Its role was to provide advice to the mayor and the Mass Housing Partnership and was not a sinister effort to control the process. If you think of it who else would you ask to advise you on what the city should do than your supporters!

Even if the media misses an opportunity for that "Gotcha" moment they still try to make it look like you did something wrong. When I was working in Lawrence, the city was implementing an urban systems transportation improvement project. Part of the design called for "neck down" features, which reduce the width of the road at strategic locations by eliminating parking and making the street more pedestrian friendly. The design went through a public hearing process and no one objected to this design feature during the hearing. During construction the elimination of parking became a concern for many citizens and the decision was made to remove some of the "neck downs". The work had already taken place so brand new sidewalks had to be ripped out and the road widened.

A Boston TV outlet visited the Lawrence Community Development office, which was in charge of the project to talk with the director about the change in design and the "wasting" of public dollars by demolishing work that had been completed and then reconstructing the street. The reporter who did not have an appointment asked to speak to the director and was told he was at a meeting outside the office. When asked when he would return the reporter was told there was no timeframe for his return. The office door for the director was open. The reporter walked over, closed the door and asked her film crew to begin taping. She then summarized the controversy and then stated at the end, "I am standing outside the office of the director of the Lawrence Community Development Department to talk with him about this waste of taxpayer dollars and to get his comments but we were told he was unavailable to talk with us."

That "Gotcha" moment is for the most part aimed at challenging your credibility but sometimes it is aimed at embarrassing you. A cousin who shares my last name was an aid to a legislator. After regular business hours she attended a gathering with other aids and legislators. Looking for a quiet place to talk, the legislator and my cousin were found by security personnel in the House Chambers. The discovery and the lack of good judgment were reported in the news media. The *Boston Globe* along with the *Boston Herald* reported that a legislator and an aid were in the House Chamber after hours and questioned the legislator specifically about the event. He apologized for using poor judgment and was discipline by leadership. While both Boston papers publish his name they both did not use her name and referred to her as an aid. However, the *Eagle Tribune* published her name along with the legislator's name and the details of the story.

A few months after the story, the *Eagle Tribune* was doing a story on the reconstruction of the Methuen Rotary at I-93 and Routes 110 and 113. A local legislator was being interviewed by the *Eagle Tribune* reporter. The Merrimack Valley Planning Commission (MVPC) prepared all the studies associated with the project and the legislator and I were working to obtain funding to advance the project. The legislator suggested to the reporter that he contact me for specific details of the project since I was the Executive Director of MVPC. The reporter said he doubted I would talk with him since he used my daughter's name in the state house article. The legislator told him that it was not my daughter who was involved in the state house issue, but a cousin. He then asked him why he put her name in the story since the other news outlets did not. He responded by telling the legislator that the editor suggested he put it in the article since she was my daughter.

Political people like me decide to lead public lives, and we lose some of our privacy because of it, but family members are what I like to call civilians. They did not decide to make their lives public, and should be excluded from "Gotcha" moments. I think the press loses some of their credibility when they look to embarrass civilians.

Newspapers believe that controversial and bad news sells papers and for the most part put these stories on the front page of the paper. If you are able to get a positive article printed in the paper it usually is found in the metro section of the paper which is located at the first fold. Politicians prefer positive stories over negative ones, but there is an element of fairness to give positive stories the same attention that negative ones receive. Newspapers have the responsibility to promote the betterment of a community and equal treatment seems fair.

Public officials seek to encourage positive press. Some believe that if they develop a rapport and friendly relationship with the press that it will lead to more positive reporting. Clearly having a cordial and collegial relationship helps during interviews, but you should not believe that it will influence their coverage. Politicians try to nurture their relationship with the press by calling them proactively and talking non-specifics and non-political issues. But inevitably the press will publish an article critical of the politician just to remind them that they are independent and just because we have conversations and some laughs doesn't mean you are not fair game.

Outside of issuing press releases with the hopes of a resulting positive article the best one can do is to wait to be contacted by the press and respond to their inquiry. You need to be accessible, but careful in talking with them because for the most part reporters who call you have written the story and are looking for quotes to verify their conclusions. This works well when you are perceived or used as an expert on the subject of the article, but can be problematic if you or your involvement is the subject of the article.

Many news organizations claim proud traditions of holding government officials and institutions accountable to the public, while politicians have raised questions about holding the press itself accountable. The news media can shape public opinion, and news organizations and journalists have a responsibility to act in the interest of the betterment of the community.

Chapter 9

"Tear Down The Wall"

One of the challenges associated with managing a large bureaucracy is convincing mangers that they are part of a team. Each manager has risen to their position through hard work and an individual journey and making sure they realize that they are not independent players in the game but are part of a team is something to strive for. Regular staff meetings are a good way of building a team approach. Managers get to meet with their colleagues on a regular basis and hear about their work efforts and their priorities. They then get opportunities to identify ways they can cooperate and communicate with their fellow managers. The CEO gets an opportunity to confirm the priorities, promote working together and provide overall bureaucracy information all at one time like changes to employee benefits, events, training and development initiatives that affect all departments.

As a firm believer in this management tool I called for monthly staff meetings. At the first meeting all were present except for the school superintendent who apologized, but had a scheduling conflict. The superintendent had many conflicts in the first few years and attended very few staff meetings. When the Methuen Charter was changed to allow for a mayor form of government the drafters of the new charter simply replaced the words town manager with mayor. The charter states that "the mayor shall supervise and direct the administration of all departments ...except for the school committee … The mayor shall be responsible for the purchasing of all supplies, materials and equipment for all departments and activities of the city, but not including food for schools, school books and other printed and audio-visual subject material, unless otherwise requested by the school committee." It was not surprising that the superintendent did not make attending mayor staff meetings a priority.

In fiscal year 2016 the school department accounted for 46% of the municipal budget. When charge backs for teacher benefits like health and retirement, police service officers, DPW services and indirect costs such as water and sewer are included the budget dedicated for school activities exceed well over 50%. Because of the charter provisions there is a budgetary wall between the municipal and school sides of government. But for practical purposes there are and should be opportunities for the municipal side and school sides of government to better cooperate and communicate.

Let's consider the functions the municipal side and the school side of government have in common. They both manage large buildings and need preventive maintenance, janitorial services and supplies. They both employ large numbers of people and need personnel management. They both need information technology and record management services. They both require legal representation. They both manage tax dollars and need to account for their use. They need to purchase fuel, electricity, food services and clerical supplies. Even the procurement of goods and services are responsibilities of both. They also have opportunities to be entrepreneurial. They can install solar panels; enter into energy saving company (ESCO) agreements and lease and share buildings to generate new revenue.

During the campaign one of the ideas I advocated for was better cooperation between the municipal and school sides of government to consider some of these obvious opportunities to be more efficient and effective. There are a few reasons why this is so difficult. The first is the city's organizational structure created through the charter, clearly separates the two sides of the government. The second is less structure and more about people. There is an inherent mistrust between the sides, one filled with jealousy, competition and turf control.

While the following episode occurred in January of 1994 it is indicative of the overall relationship between the city and school side that even exists today. The school department runs an after-school program called the School Age Child Care Center and accepts tuition payments from parents to run latchkey activities and care of the students until their parent pick them up. Revenue collected goes into a revolving account and the school department uses the proceeds to pay for teachers and other personnel to run the program. At the end of the fiscal year all funds not expended go into the city general fund as dictate by state law and any excess goes into free cash.

At the end of the fiscal year the superintendent made an agreement with the town auditor and town manager to transfer $40,000 back into the revolving fund to continue paying expenditures to run the center. However, in the new fiscal year the funds were not transferred to the revolving fund and the program was running a deficit. The city refused to pay invoices out of the account because of the deficit and the superintendent approached the school committee to transfer some funds into the account so as to not have to close the program.

In explaining the need for the funds, the superintendent said, "The same town accountant who took that money is now telling us we have no money and can't pay our bills." With that the rhetoric became critical. One school committeeman said, "The money move was the city's worst I have seen in my 20 years on the school committee." He went on to say, "This is a blatant example of fiscal irresponsibility on the part of town hall" and suggested "we should hire an auditor." Another school committeeman said the city "stole" the money for the school department and that the city was blaming the deficit on the business administrator. He then stated, "The town accountant and his little friends are playing games over there and have tried to make the school department look stupid for the last time."

The superintendent ended the discussion by saying "I heard rumors last spring, as you do in Methuen, they're going to take your money". He continued "I was assured at that time the money would be re-appropriated to the account and our agreement was welched upon". (20)

A set of school committee members attended the next city council meeting and after more colorful rhetoric the issue was resolve. The town accountant and then town manager cannot appropriate funds so the transfer could not happen without an appropriation of funds by the city council. I recommended that the city council consider appropriating the $40,000 from free cash since it had been placed into that account. Once appropriated the issue was resolved. This type of mistrust is shared on both sides so negotiating agreements to bring better cooperation between the two sides is extremely difficult.

One way to bring change is to change the dynamic. The dynamic here is to change the relationship between the city and the school department by having the mayor on the school committee and also serving as chairperson. The opportunity to propose this change came in 1996. After two years in office I identified three changes that could be made to the charter that would give the mayor more authority to better manage the city. Working with the city council we placed a charter changing referendum on the November 1996 ballot. If approved by the voters the mayor would have authority to hire personnel below middle management level, place department heads on three-year terms and allow the mayor to serve on the school committee as its chair.

The school committee change drew the most attention during the referendum debate. Two existing school committee members wrote op-ed pieces for the local news outlets, both opposed to the change. The school committee members questioned the motivation for the change feeling there was no public outcry so why change.

The vast majority of citizens are not engaged in the day to day operations of the city. They look for their political leaders to represent them and suggest ways the government can be improved to deliver the services they want and come to expect. Having the mayor play a role (one vote out of seven members) in the oversight of over half of the city's budget would seem to be a legitimate recommendation from their mayor.

They questioned why the mayor should be on a "policy making" committee with no other authority. While the 1993 Education Reform Act passed by the Massachusetts legislature and signed by the governor did take authority from the school committee and placed more of it in the hands of the superintendent the school committee still votes on the school department budget recommended by the superintendent. Although the mayor needs to ask the citizens to fund the school budget, the mayor has no say in how funds are spent without this change. With this change the mayor would have the ability to discuss spending priorities just like other school committee members.

They both expressed concern that the mayor would attempt to "take over the superintendent job" and be the chief administrative officer of the school system. By statute this is not a possibility. The superintendent has been given the authority to manage the school department per the Education Reform Act and the mayor cannot and should not be the chief administrative officer of the school department. The mayor involvement on the school committee will improve communication between the superintendent and the municipal side. The issue with the revolving fund could have been handled bureaucratically if the mayor knew of the issue. The rancor and accusations would have not been made and the relationship between the sides would not have been strained.

There was also a suggestion that the mayor's presence on the school committee would politicize the school department by allowing political interference with the operations of the school system. While it is true the mayor is a political person so are the other school committee members and the potential to politicize exists today. In some ways the Education Reform Act insulated the superintendent from this possibility because the superintendent controls hiring and administrative decisions not the school committee.

The potential benefits of the mayor being on the school committee outweigh the perceived negatives. It gives the government the opportunity to act in a unified manner. One constant complaint is that the city side and school side negotiate with the unions independently without any unified strategy for management rights, benefits and salary increases. The mayor can share with the school committee and the superintendent the standards and parameters being offered to the city side of government and this information can be considered during school department negotiations. This would go a long way to reduce the competition between the unions on both sides of government. And most importantly it gives the mayor more fiscal oversight, which citizens expect, and it brings the potential of improved cooperation and coordination between the two sides of the government.

The charter change referendum was held on November 5, 1996, the same day of a presidential election so the turnout was significantly higher than municipal elections. The change in the charter was approved 8,690 to 7,538. The Superintendent attended my first staff meeting in January 1997.

I believe having the mayor on the school committee improved the relationship between the two sides of government. It definitely improved communications. After the Columbine school shooting the superintendent, police chief and myself met on a number of occasions to compare notes on students that were being monitored for problem behavior by the high school police service officer and by the high school administration and developed procedures in case of the need to evacuate the high school. We coordinated the leasing of the field house to a religious gathering that was predicted to attract thousands of people. We were also able to coordinate our efforts to build three new K through 8 schools. As you can imagine a significant endeavor which required coordination on financing, design, programming, construction and temporary school buildings.

It did not however lead to any significant combined management of similar functions I had hoped for and had advocated for during the election. While we had created a structure to discuss opportunities the need to focus my "political capital" on the management and construction of the new schools took priority. I believe my successors have had some limited success in this area. It has been limited because the school committee still views themselves as independent.

In the 19th century, Massachusetts made school committees independent of local governments. It became a model across the country and exists even today. In some communities there are even separate tax rates for school and municipal services. I think there is a need to change this approach if we are to bring any significant efficiency to municipal management. There is no fiscal accountability placed on the school committee as there is with the mayor and the city council. If they returned to separate tax rates for school and municipal sides of government then the school committees could be held fiscally responsible and would be incentivized to find efficiencies. The potential for separate tax rates is not likely considering the Education Reform Act and the net school spending requirements and direct and indirect spending categories. Is there an alternative?

I believe the best alternative would be to reconfigure the traditional school committee. The City of Boston reconfigured their school committee by a 1991 public referendum vote. The 13-member elected Boston School Committee had been criticized as being ineffective. Many of its members were perceived to be interested in using the school committee as a stepping stone for future political advancement and out of touch with the administration. The referendum created a seven-member school board appointed by the mayor after approval by a nominating committee of specified stakeholders. (21) The appointed school committee would be responsible for hiring a superintendent, set policy for the district and approve the district's annual budget. The school superintendent is part of the Mayor's cabinet.

While this certainly is a departure from the traditional approach and improves the ability to break down barriers between the two sides of government, I think accountability, particularly in a strong mayor form of government as in Boston, may be too focused on the mayor. I think there is a need for more checks and balances.

I would propose that the school committee be eliminated and that the city council be given the responsibilities of the school committee. The city council would approach their responsibilities with a broader view of the needs for both sides of government. They would still be accountable for overseeing the school department to the voters just like the school committee is now, but they would also be held fiscally responsible whereas the school committee is not. The mayor would be responsible for selecting a superintendent subject to the approval of the city council. The superintendent would still have the independence required in the Education Reform Act to manage the day to day activities of the school department without interference from the mayor and city council.

Chapter 10

"How Would You Like A Rat On Your Lawn"

Unions organize and advocate for workers from salary, to work rules, and to grievances. They attempt to resolve workforce issues and are a voice for employees. The debate around trash privatization is a prime example. At the public hearing to discuss privatization the union steward admitted he was personally opposed to the privatization of trash pickup, but his members were in favor of the privatization because they did not like the work and conditions.

All too often the unions seem to be the voice of a minority of the employees. As in many organizations most of the workers are conscientious and attempt to do the job they were hired to do. While not scientific I believe 5% of the workforce tries to use the rules and regulations to personally benefit themselves and the union is under a perception that it needs to represent all the employees and is the voice to defend abuses.

In 2008 a firefighter in the City of Boston claimed he injured his back while walking down a set of stairs at a fire station. However, while out on leave because of the injury he trained and competed in a national body building competition and actually placed 8th in the competition and then applied for disability retirement. Sighting this activity, the Boston Fire Commissioner recommended to the Boston Retirement

Board that they deny the disability retirement claim. The commissioner then removed him from injury related leave, which is tax exempt, and placed him on regular sick leave, which is taxable. The union appealed the decision to remove him from injured in the line of duty to sick leave status. The City of Boston ended up terminating his employment after they demanded the return to work and he declined. (22)

In my first year as mayor, the fire chief came in to inform me he was struggling to stay within his overtime budget. He actually told me that "this department does not practice fiscal responsibility." I told him "well it is about to start now." One of the uses of overtime is to fill in for firefighters who are out of work due to work related injuries. To better understand the status of the firefighters out on injured reserve I asked Chief Clark to review with me the injuries of each firefighter and prognosis for return. One firefighter injured his hand and had not been seen by our doctor for almost six months, I asked Chief Clark to have the firefighter examined by our doctor to determine when he may be able to return to work. He returned the next day to inform me that the firefighter was in Florida. I told him to have the firefighter return to Methuen and see our doctor. The union protested the order to return to Massachusetts.

Another driver of overtime was filling in for lieutenants that called in sick. The Methuen firefighter contract contained a provision for minimum manning. Minimum manning required that 18 firefighters would have to be on duty for each shift to ensure sufficient staff was present to man all firefighting equipment that may be needed to fight a fire. The full complement for a shift was 24. That meant if seven firefighters called in sick one firefighter would have to be called in to cover a position, so we could maintain the minimum number of firefighters. However, there was a nuance. If one of the firefighters who called in sick was a lieutenant, then despite room under the minimum manning provision a lieutenant would need to be called in to replace the lieutenant. It resulted in mandatory overtime every time a lieutenant called in sick.

In an attempt to get the overtime budget back on track I instructed the chief to elevate the most senior firefighter on a shift to lieutenant rank, pay the differential, and avoid calling in a lieutenant and pay overtime wages. Needless to say, the union was outraged and filed a grievance on the move. I denied the grievance but offered to forgo this temporary shift promotion provided the overtime budget was within prorated budget compliance.

However, these kinds of abuses happen in all departments. Another example is a DPW worker who was out on disability due to a shoulder injury. She was on workers comp and had been out for over two years claiming her shoulder was not sufficiently healed to return to work. Feeling that there may be abuse I asked our workers comp agent to have an investigator follow the worker for a few days. The investigator returned with a video of the worker running down the beach holding her arms above her shoulders flying a kite with her children. Sighting this video, we discontinued her injury related leave and asked her to return to work. The union opposed this move and unfortunately the court agreed and returned her to workers comp status sighting that the activity did not prove she did not still feel sufficient pain not to return to work. We then decided to support a disability retirement to remove her from the budget and replace her.

Through these appeals the unions were condoning this kind of abuse at the expense of the majority of workers. It also undermines the future of unions in the public sector and even the continued employment of their members. All too often unions oppose efforts to improve municipal services or save tax dollars with reforms.

Back in 2009, Dr. Barry Bluestone, the Dean of the School of Social Science, Urban Affairs, and Public Policy at Northeastern University, wrote an op-ed piece entitled "A Future for Public Union", for the *Boston Globe*. While working his way through college on a Ford assembly line he was a member of the UAW. He talks about the demise of the UAW going from 1.5 million members in 1960 to as few as 465,000 members today. He sighted them for "insisting on job classifications and work rules that undermined efficiency and compromised the industry's competitiveness." He goes on by asking:

> *"Will public-sector unions follow the same path? Nationwide, these unions represent over 35 percent of federal, state, and local employees, roughly the same as in 1980. Over the years, they have won improved wages*

and benefits for their members. Yet the leaders of many of these unions, particularly in Massachusetts, seem to be setting the stage for the same kind of deterioration we see in unions like the UAW.

Teachers unions refuse to make changes in work practices that could help improve the chances of children succeeding in school. Police unions fight against lowering the cost of details at construction sites. The MBTA union and others representing transport workers lobby vociferously against reforming the state's transportation system. Municipal unions refuse to permit their local communities to join the Group Insurance Commission that would save their towns millions without compromising the quality of their members' medical care.

As a result, between 2000 and 2008, the price of state and local public services has increased by 41 percent nationally compared with 27 percent in private services. Even in the face of the worst fiscal crisis in decades, many state and local union leaders refuse to consider a wage freeze that could help preserve more of their members' jobs.

Such action is rapidly losing the support public-sector unions need to survive. Union leaders may think that by working diligently to elect friendly public officials, they can fend off the day of reckoning. But that day is fast approaching. Citizens, and ultimately their elected representatives, will increasingly object to tax increases to pay for what they see as bloated union contracts and poor public service.

Ultimately, new ways will be found to provide public services to circumvent public unions. Non-union charter schools will proliferate, not to reduce teachers' salaries or benefits but to avoid a plethora of work rules that make school reform difficult. Public services will be privatized with private contractors hired to pick up trash (in addition to recycling), to guard prisoners, and perhaps even to fight fires. Public highways may be sold off. The result: public-sector unions will see their memberships and their influence decline.

This will be a tragedy. To move in a different direction, we need to think about a new "grand bargain" between public-sector unions and government. Union leaders in the state need to consider ways to work collaboratively with public officials so as to offer quality public services at a reasonable cost to the taxpayer while preserving union jobs for their members." (23)

Bluestone's predictions are coming true. We already discussed trash privatization and in 2016 the MBTA has begun to privatize cash counting, fare collection, marketing and warehousing logistics and management. The MBTA is also exploring privatization of bus maintenance and transit police dispatching as well.

It is not surprising that the MBTA is exploring privatization. The Boston Carmen's union local 589, the largest bargaining unit at the MBTA, has traditionally resisted any reform or service improvements. A recent effort to reform the employee pension benefit is a prime example. The MBTA union had negotiated retirement benefits that allowed employees to retire after 23 years of service and despite any age requirements retire with 63% of the employees three highest years of earnings average including 100% health coverage. Think of it, an employee who starts work at the MBTA at say twenty years old, could retire at forty-three with 63% of their salary and 100% health insurance for the rest of their life! The benefit, which is one of the best in the country, is a major cost factor at the MBTA and drains institutional knowledge from the workforce. Despite major MBTA budgetary problems the Carmen's Union opposed any reform. Although the retirement benefits were ultimately changed they still exceed the benefits allowed to other State employees because of the Union's opposition.

Even efforts to modify service or look for ways to improve service were opposed by the unions. When I led the effort to solicit input from the residents of Jamaica Plain to possibly restore green line service to Jamaica Plain the unions came to the public meeting and literally disrupted the proceedings. During the public solicitation phase of the meeting the President and Business Agent for the Carmen's Union James McDougal mocked me and our team for coming to the neighborhood without promises to restore service that was discontinued many years earlier. After introducing himself he proceeded to question our motives for even being there. "You sir, who are you to come to the neighborhood and tell these people they can't have this service. The Carmen's Union supports restoring service so you should just restore the service and stop this process." The crowd erupted with applause as McDougal played to their emotions. The meeting became useless as the attendees refused to provide positive input into the process and began to criticize the MBTA and praised the union for supporting the neighborhood. The union had an opportunity to be part of making the meeting productive and useful by helping the residents articulate their needs and concerns but they decided to oppose any improvement or discussion that made the MBTA more responsive to their customers.

It is possible to move unions in a different direction through negotiations. During one set of negotiations with Methuen's ten bargaining units, I was able to include performance evaluations into the contracts. This may sound like a routine requirement, but this was monumental at the time. Not only were we able to include performance evaluations as a management right, but we were also able to attach raises to the results.

Normally when salaries are negotiated employees all receive the same raise. Many public employees complained about this practice. Employees know who is productive and who is not and when they see those employees that do not have the same work ethics than they do receive the same raise they feel cheated. Using this feeling we negotiated a 3% increase for those employees that received a good evaluation and a 2% for those who had an evaluation that called for performance improvement. In this case the unions decided they wanted to be part of improving the "quality of public services".

While this was clearly a success the task I hated most while mayor was negotiating new union contracts. The unions are always looking for more compensation and benefits for their members and the municipality is looking for a compensation and benefit package that will not overburden the taxpayer. Most people focus on the salary wage increases when estimating contract impacts but over time the compensation package has gotten much more complex. There are many items that have been added to contracts over time. There are stipends for longevity. There are sick leave buy back provisions. There are pension enhancement benefits. There are clothing and cleaning allowances. There are stipends to maintain professional certifications like Emergency Management Technician (EMT). The municipal contribution to health care is a negotiated item in contracts. Sometimes these allowances and stipends are percentages of salaries and salary increases trigger stipend increases. There are also work conditions and rules that are negotiated like hours of work, hours in the office, compensatory time, holiday pay, overtime minimums, having your birthday off, and minimum manning requirements. All these items can have a significant impact on municipal budgets.

These non-salary items were added by both sides of the negotiation table. On the union side it was an attempt to get more compensation for their members and in some cases different compensation items that other union may not have. The DPW union would always try to maintain in their contract Lafayette day as a holiday. Lafayette once stayed in Methuen and his birthday became a contractual holiday. Having this random day as a holiday brought some management problems and overtime requirements. When I tried to negotiate it out of the contract I was sternly told that they rather take less money than give up their unique holiday.

On the municipal side management would try to shield the true cost of the contract from the voters by including some of these non-cash items. Work conditions and rules do not always have a direct budget cost item like an extra holiday or your birthday off. Even increases in health care costs are somewhat hidden in the municipal budget because of different health care plans offered. Municipalities also liked to limit impact on the budget by giving less costly items than salary increases. This was typical for health insurance contribution percentages, particularly when health care costs were less than they are today. Methuen always maintained a low percentage of employer contribution at 68%. However, some communities, like Peabody, increased their percentage all the way to 100%. Today because of the high cost of health insurance communities have been trying to reduce their contribution. Peabody is down to 85% but it is very difficult to negotiate changes. Once a union has negotiated something for its members they rarely change it unless they are somehow incentivized to do so.

Because of all this complexity it is hard to evaluate the affects a compensation package will have on the budget. During negotiations you need to regularly go to the finance office and ask them to re-calculate the impact the contract will have on the budget. You also need the department heads to identify management rights that would help them better manage their department. These items need to be put on the table during negotiations as bargaining item for increases in the compensation package. An example is the performance evaluation requirement. The mayor in conjunction with the finance director needs to determine how much the community can afford to increase the employee compensation package. Always keeping in mind that this is one bargaining unit and that what you give to one you will most likely need to give to the other. Obviously, there are variances because of the unique nature of some departments but the pattern does become the foundation for negotiation.

You begin the negotiation hoping that you can find some common ground and build consensus around a contract that benefits both the employees and the municipalities. I was fond of telling the unions that if Methuen was doing well financially then we would share that success with the employees. The unions were fond of asking "how much do you respect your employees?" While I was able to settle some contracts amicably inevitably there were some contracts that were not.

The unions use a number of tactics to force concessions. One of their favorite tactics is to have their members picket. They picket many venues where the municipal leaders are present. I had the unique privilege of being picketed by the Methuen police and fire unions as well as the Lawrence police and fire unions. The Massachusetts Mayors Association (MMA) holds monthly meetings with the mayors from across the state. The cities take turns hosting these meeting and I offered to host a meeting at the Methuen Organ Hall. The Organ Hall was built by Edward Searles, a local philanthropist, in 1909 and the interior architecture rivals music halls in Boston. I thought it was an opportunity to show off this magnificent building to the other mayors in Massachusetts and would be a good venue for a MMA meeting. Contract negotiation with the Methuen police and fire were contentious. It was my first contract with them and there was certainly testing going on, on both sides. The Lawrence mayor was also in the mist of hard negotiations with the Lawrence police and fire. All four unions decided to picket the event.

As the mayors arrived they were confronted with the picket lines. As mayors they were not intimidated by this tactic and when the President of the MMA, Mayor Barrett from North Adams, started the meeting he commented "While we all don't know the specifics of your disagreement with the unions, we are confident you are on the right side. Think on the bright side they probably have ensured your re-election."

It can be unsettling when crossing picket lines. While you accept the right to picket and are not swayed by the occurrence it can be upsetting. One venue the fire union decided to picket was my initial Employee Appreciation Day event. Annually, I would hold an event where I recognized perfect and near perfect attendance and significant year anniversaries like twenty or twenty-five years of service to the community. We would have a breakfast for those employees being recognized and gave them a token of appreciation. To be honest crossing the picket line to attend this event aggravated me. I wanted to do something nice for the employees and the day was disrupted by the picketing. While I refused to show my displeasure, it bothered me more than they realized.

Another tactic used by unions is intimidation. One negotiation that became contentious was the school nurse contract. After the charter change I was assigned by the school committee to help the superintendent negotiate this contract. The nurses union wanted all registered nurses to be paid at the same rate as teachers. The school department's position was that most of the nurses were not required to have the education and certification requirements equivalent to teachers. Many of the nurses did not have college degrees since they were hired before this requirement was standard. The counter to the unions on this issue was that all nurses that had equivalent education and certifications would be place on the same pay scale as teachers, but those who did not would be on a lower pay scale. As mentioned unions sometimes decide they need to represent all their members equally, so the counter was rejected.

At a regularly scheduled school committee meeting the nurses' union attended and organized parents sympathetic to their position to attend as well. At the beginning of each meeting the school committee would have public participation. During public participation the nurses' union steward addressed the school committee and reiterated their position and demanded support from the school committee. The parents followed with their support and antidotal stories of how important the nurses were to their school. After an hour of testimony, the crowd concluded their remarks' and asked for the committee response. As chair of the school committee I thanked them for attending and told them the committee would take their comments into consideration. I then called for the next item on the agenda and continued our meeting without commenting further on their position. Union negotiations are not held in a public setting and I was not going to allow the committee to be intimated by the crowd. Confused the crowd started to leave slowly at first thinking that the committee would discuss the issue. Once they realized that there would be no further discussion on the issue they left. The school committee held fast to their position and the contract reflected the school department position.

Verbal intimidation is another tactic unions use to negotiate. The Methuen police union asked the Teamsters Local 25 out of Charlestown to represent them during negotiations. It always struck me as odd that a law enforcement union would hire this Teamster bargaining group. Teamsters Local 25 were notorious bullies and corrupt. As late as 2015, members of

Local 25 were indicted on conspiracy to extort and attempted extortion of a television production company in order to obtain no-work jobs for fellow Teamsters. (24)   Based on my experience with them this is just the latest example of their style of negotiations. I would typically ask each department head to meet with the union and present the city's position, both management issues and financial compensation. I would give the department head direction but would not participate in the initial meetings. The intent was to better understand the differences between the unions and the city and report back to me. I tried to become the closer once we knew how far we were apart and what might get us to an agreement.

At the initial meeting the chief and the city attorney met with the teamsters. Chief Bruce MacDougall is a well-liked, amicable person and professionally presented the city's position. The teamsters mocked the offer and would not present their position as a counter and they demanded to meet with the mayor. I had to laugh when the city attorney told me that the chief had made available coffee and cookies for the meeting but after being berated and shouted at by the teamsters he declared "That's it no more cookies for them!"

When the teamsters arrived at our meeting there were very little pleasantries. They started the meeting by complaining about the chief. They were derogatory and felt the chief disrespected them and his police officers. Their language was harsh and loud. They were dominating the meeting with their negative talk; I slammed my hand on the table to get their attention and shouted, "Stop!" I told them if they had any

137

complaints about our position that they should address them to me and that the chief was acting on my directions. I then informed them that the chief had been in the department as a police officer and a ranking officer before he became chief and their "respect" comments were totally off base and groundless. I was not going to allow them to insult the chief and dictate the tone of negotiations.

At this point they aimed their comments at me. "You know mayor when we negotiate with someone like you we need to let you know this will not be a painless process. We are prepared to have trucks drive through your community with bull horns telling everyone you are unfair to labor." They then said, "How would you like to find a rat on your lawn." I told them "You need to do what you need to do and I will do what I need to do." I then informed them that the meeting was over and that there would not be another meeting until they presented their offer.

Police and fire unions are not incentivized to settle contract disputes. Chapter 589 of the acts of 1987 created the Joint Labor and Management Committee (JLMC). The purpose of the committee is to encourage the parties of collective bargaining disputes between municipalities and police officers and firefighter to resolve these disputes. The committee forces the municipality to agree to procedures such as mediation and arbitration to settle the dispute. Unions are empowered by this requirement to refrain from negotiation and wait for an imposed solution. There is a feeling that if the unions ask for a "great" contract and the Municipality offers a "fair" contract that the JLMC will result in a "good" contract, so why settle?

There is some truth to this scenario. While the JLMC does not use the words "binding arbitration" for all practical purposes the arbitration is binding. The mayor is required to support the arbitration decision, but the decision is subject to appropriation by the city council. In theory the city council can reject the decision, so it is not technically binding, but in reality, it is very rare for a city council to reject a JLMC arbitrated contract. The mayor is required to support the arbitration decision even if he or she is opposed. The system is rigged for the unions and they know it.

As you can imagine the negotiation with the teamsters went to the JLMC. We were required to go into mediation. Mediation was intense shuttle diplomacy between me, the city solicitor and the police chief in my office and the teamsters and the police union on the other side of the building in the city solicitor's office. The mediator would negotiate an offer and then bring it to the other party and go back and forth working to bring us together. In the end we settled the contract. While I opposed the ultimate settlement, I recommended approval to the city council as required but stated in my recommendation that I believed that the contract would require us to raise taxes more than discussed to balance the budget. The city council approved the contract unanimously.

Another tactic used by unions is to call for a strike. This is rare since public employee are prohibited from striking in

Massachusetts, but in September of 1988 both the Lowell and Peabody teachers unions failed to report to school at the beginning of the school year. I was working in Peabody when the strike occurred and Mayor Torigian asked management to volunteer to fill in for the 400 teachers that failed to show up. I filled in at the Brown School and kept the children engaged by talking about the city government. The union was asking for 9% a year over a three-year period. The city's counter was 5.5% a year over the three years. Torigian told the press that the teacher's union came to the table with the 9% request and after three years of negotiations did not move once during the discussions. When you compound the raise requested it would amount to an increase of over 42% over the three years. (25)

Torigian was upset that the teachers approached negotiations with a rigid stance. He also recognized that this was a unique situation since it was illegal to strike and felt that there was a learning opportunity for other municipalities on how to deal with a strike. He produced a video that highlighted efforts the city took to end the strike. The video included steps the city attorneys took to get an injunction to force the teachers to return to work and the need to win the media battle with the union to ensure the public knew the details of the city's offer and the impact it would have on taxes and on the municipal budget.

The current municipal financial structure threatens the ability of a community to provide municipal services and is unsustainable if raises and benefits were granted at the rates requested by the unions. In 1982 Proposition 2½ was approved by statewide referendum. Proposition 2 ½ capped the amount of property taxes a community can assess to 2½ % of the total cash value of all taxable property in the community. A community's allowable property tax levy, which is the major source of revenue for all communities, cannot increase by more than 2½ % of the prior year's taxable property (which is its levy ceiling) plus new growth. With their reliance on property taxes and the limits placed on this revenue source from Proposition 2 ½, most municipalities turn to state aid and economic development to expand their property tax base to keep pace with the increase cost of providing services. Without state aid proposition 2 ½ does not work. State aid is not as reliable as municipal leaders would like it to be. During the "Great Recession" of 2009 state aid was cut to local communities and communities had to cut their budgets and layoff personnel. Communities need to be more efficient, innovative and consider regionalization to reduce costs to pay for the salaries, benefits, pensions and post pension benefits the unions demand during negotiations. Unions need to consider a paradigm shift as suggested by Dr. Bluestone. The future of municipalities, the unions and the jobs for their members is on the line.

Chapter 11

"There Is More Too It"

The responsibilities of mayor are much broader than what is spelled out in the city charter. The charter describes in detail the executive authority and duties the mayor has in governing the city. It describes the mayor's role in supervising and directing all departments and employees, negotiating and executing contracts, maintaining and determine use of all municipal buildings, and the purchasing of all goods and services for the city. For all practical purposes it is the bylaws the mayor uses to manage the city.

But there is more to the job than just managing the city. The mayor is the leader of the community and represents the city in good times and in bad. Each mayor individually defines this role so the approach, the outcome and the effectiveness is different from one administration to another.

I outlined my priorities and vision during my election campaign. When I announced my candidacy one of the constant comments I heard was that people liked living in Methuen but disliked its negative reputation and image. They liked the school system, the recreational facilities, the historic buildings, the reasonable taxes and the nice neighborhoods but disliked the "bad blood" politics associated with Methuen. Council meetings were legendary. Councilors were known for name calling, grandstanding, temper tantrums and even physical confrontations.

In response to this reputation one councilor proposed a "be nice" resolution to suggest civil discourse during council meeting. After passage, this same councilor was the first to violate the resolution and his violation received national media attention! After a heated meeting one councilor closed the door hard when leaving the meeting and hit another councilor in the face and blooded his nose. Even their decisions were known as controversial ranging from hiring a town manager with no town government administration experience and a shady past, suspending rules to facilitate purchases outside of procurement standards and paying for invoices without sufficient documentation. So, it was easy to propose that we needed to improve the image of the City.

While good government in itself can promote a good image, the situation called for an image overhaul plan. I thought the best way to design this plan was to focus on a community pride campaign and strengthening the confidence people had in the town government.

The community pride campaign was aimed at promoting a sense of community. I called it "Methuen on the Move". It could have been called "I like Methuen" or "Methuen the place to Be" but I needed a slogan that would suggest we were moving forward. I wanted to engage the community in the development of the campaign and decided to ask the high school students to weigh in on the slogan and create a logo through a competition. The students embraced the "Methuen on the Move" slogan and through the competition selected a logo that formed the letter "M" using the turrets and historic walls built at the turn of the twentieth century, which are prevalent throughout the community.

With a citizen steering committee, we developed a series of activities to promote the campaign. I raised private funds from the business sector to fund the activities. "Methuen on the Move bumper stickers and signs were purchased and distributed to citizens. We used "Earth Day" to organize a community wide cleanup campaign. T-shirts and hats with the slogan and logo imprinted on them were provided for those participating. After the morning cleanup, a cookout was held at a community park and awards were given out to the organizers.

Another activity was to solicit sponsors to plant flowers at traffic islands throughout the city. Businesses, citizens and even some councilors sponsored islands and their participation was recognized with "Methuen on the Move" signs at each location with their sponsorship identified. A partnership was formed with the Methuen Board of Trade and the many veterans groups in the City to develop the American Flag Program. The program involved placing American Flags on utility poles throughout the downtown on significant holidays such as, Memorial Day, Fourth of July, Labor Day, Flag Day and Veterans Day.

To promote the community pride campaign and the positive things happening in the community I hosted a local cable television show called "Methuen on the Move". Each month I would host a show and invite department heads, or state and federal officials to be my guest and inform the citizens of what was happening in the city and how some of the citizens could benefit from these efforts. We obviously used the venue to promote the yearly activities associated with the "Methuen on the Move" campaign.

Strengthening the confidence people had in the government was the other element of the image overhaul plan. During the mayoral campaign I referred to bringing a "code of ethics" to city hall. I thought imposing my code of ethics on the employees of the city would not be effective. It would be like "who is this new guy coming in and telling us we are not professional and telling us how we should act, and suggesting we do not respect the citizens." The employees needed to be part of defining the city's mission and setting goals and objectives for their work.

During the 1990s a popular management technique used by organizations was Total Quality Management (TQM). TQM is an organization-wide effort to install and make permanent a climate in which an organization continuously improves its ability to deliver high-quality products and services to customers. It is driven by engaging the employees in developing methods that can make them more responsive and productive in doing their jobs. It became popular because of its success in Japan where W. Edwards Deming used the techniques to make Japan one of the most productive economies in the world. (26)

I approached the CEOs of Lawrence, Andover and North Andover and collectively we received a State grant to introduce TQM to our communities. Each community was awarded $9,000. We hired a facilitating TQM consultant and held a joint kick-off meeting at Merrimack College. The employees from the communities learned about the concept. I then arranged for an offsite venue with our employees to begin the process of generating the mission statement for the government and the goals and objectives that would help them meet that mission. I attended all the meetings and helped facilitate and direct the effort. There was a sense of ownership from the employees and their code of standards was adopted in the form of a Vision statement and a Mission statement. This statement is still displayed at City Hall Today.

Our Vision

Methuen is a community where residents young and old are proud to live and work. It is served by a government that promotes trust and integrity through efficient and effective operations, dedicated to quality, responsiveness, cooperation and innovation.

Our Vision

We the employees of Methuen will continually strive to improve the quality of life in our community by working to increase confidence and pride in every neighborhood. This shall be accomplished by:

- *Interacting with the community and responding to its needs.*
- *Equitably developing and managing rules and regulations.*
- *Maintaining a level of professionalism through accessibility and accountability.*
- *Practicing sound fiscal management.*

- *Improving cooperation and respect between government bodies and departments.*
- *Promoting and preserving Methuen's historical and natural beauty.*
- *Enhancing the educational process to encourage life-long learning.*
- *Providing a high-quality recreation and park system.*
- *Insuring a safe and healthy environment in which to live and work.*

Once established we continuously reinforced the effort with training. The training included conflict of interest, how to deal with difficult people, proper phone etiquette and other customer improvement techniques. I also tried to recognize employees and established an employee of the month program and a yearly Employee Appreciation Day where we provide breakfast and recognized with a small token perfect and near perfect attendance and years of service to the community. While the recognition was small in some respect you could tell employees appreciated the recognition. This appreciation was shown by the fact that the number of employees with perfect and near perfect attendance increase every year from the inception of the program.

It is hard to measure the success of these image building efforts because it requires you to hear from residents if their perspective of their community has changed or has been improved. There was, however, an opportunity to survey residents about their feelings over the last two years of my term. The city's voting system was old and needed to be replaced. It was a punch hole system and it was difficult to maintain the system. The city purchased a new system that scanned ballots and sped up the counting time and brought more reliability to the process. This new system gave us an opportunity to use the system for something other than an election. On an annual basis the city clerk would send a census form to each household and ask residents to return the form to the clerk's office. Over the last two years of my administration we were able to include a survey to gauge residents' satisfaction with the city government. The questions included reference to the many city departments and to provide scores ranging from excellent, to good, to fair, and to poor. The response was significant in that the clerk receive over 5,000 surveys. All the departments received good scores of at least 90% excellent or good. I believe our image building efforts were a success.

Through my six years as mayor I was continually reminded how important the mayor is to a community. At first, I perceived the attention as just notoriety. When I accompanied my wife to do the weekly grocery shopping I was always stopped by constituents asking about an issue or asking me for some help. My wife learned pretty quickly that if she wanted to finish the shopping in a timely manner she would have to continue going up and down the aisle without me since I would have to spend time talking with folks. While you would expect the mayor to be recognized in the community I learned pretty early that you are always in the public's eye. If I went to a meeting in Boston I would be greeted by people who would say "hello Mr. Mayor." I took my family to a Red Sox game and during the game a resident came down to our seats and said hello and also mentioned he had a daughter who was looking for a teaching job in Methuen. I went to Washington D.C. for a number of meetings and was recognized in the hotel and greeted and while walking from one meeting to another I was recognized again to "hello Mr. Mayor." How far can you go? In my only vacation away from Methuen I went to Aruba with my wife and while walking along the beach I heard "hello Mr. Mayor!" I guess it is a small world after all.

It wasn't just the adults that wanted access to the mayor; the children were interested as well. The New England Revolution, the professional soccer team, wanted to promote their sport and their team and declared it Revolution Soccer Day in Methuen. Members of the team and the team mascot came to one of the schools to commemorate soccer day in Methuen. I attended the event and welcomed the team members to Methuen and introduce them before they talked with the students. After they spoke they offered to sign autographs for those who wanted them. The children lined up for the autographs and to my surprise they formed another line asking for my autograph. Unsure they would even know who I was I decided to sign each autograph with Mayor Dennis DiZoglio.

This interest level with the children continued throughout the six years. I regularly met with students who were touring city hall. I firmly believe that government is a mystery to most folks and they are not sure what it does or how it works.

When the students met with me I would introduce myself and ask them "what do you think the city does for you on a daily basis?" The students that came to city hall ranged from the 5th to the 8th grade. Regardless of the grade the response to my question was met with blank stares, unless they had visited before. With no responses I would ask "where did you come from before this tour?" They would all shout out "school." I responded by saying "who makes the school available to you?" With a slight hesitation they would say "the city?" I would respond "Yes! And if there is a fire in your neighborhood who do you call?" They responded by saying "the fire department." I said, "Who makes the fire department available to you?" They responded …"the city does." I would continue with this line of questioning asking about whom they would call if they saw a crime, or who cuts the grass at the play grounds they use, or who supplies the water they drink. I believe they left city hall knowing more about what the city does than even their parents knew.

One of the events I would never miss was a graduation ceremony for the DARE program. The Drug Abuse Resistance Education (DARE) program was run by the police department and was funded by tobacco tax revenue and was intended to discourage young people from smoking and abusing drugs. At the graduation we would have a guest motivational speaker who would encourage the students to remember their training and resist smoking or drugs. One effective speaker was a gentleman who lost his larynxes due to cancer from smoking. He used a voice box to speak but when he started his comments he would play a recording of a radio show he once hosted. He had a professional sounding voice for radio and after the recording stopped he would then talk using his voice box and would say "this is what I sound like today." The children were shocked to hear the difference. I would close the ceremony before diplomas were handed out by asking what each one wanted to do when they grew up. Many responded a baseball player, a firefighter or policeman. I joked with them that not one of them wanted to be mayor! I then told them "if you smoke or abuse drugs you cannot realize your future. You can't be a firefighter or a policeman or a sports star or anything else you want to be if you destroy your health by smoking or abusing drugs." There has been criticism of the DARE program and claims that it is not effective and in fact it has been eliminated from many communities' curriculum but I believe it was a good program to set a foundation for children to know the detrimental effects of abusing drugs, alcohol and smoking.

The role of Chief Ceremonial Officer (CCO) is played by the mayor. It is not specifically referenced in the city charter. As mentioned the charter was changed to create a mayor form of government by inserting the word mayor where the town manager was referenced. The mayor is much more visible in the community than the town manager and is the highest ranking elected official in the community and the responsibility of CCO falls on the mayor. Everyone and I mean everyone, invited the mayor to be part of their event. The events ranged from kicking off the soapbox derby for the boy scouts, to participating in an event at a church fair, to manning the phones at a scholar telethon, to attending a PTO fundraiser, to throwing out the first pitch at the start of a softball or baseball season, to making a cameo appearance in the local production of *the Sound of Music*, to attending neighborhood events on National Night Out Day, to awarding the mayor's trophy at the antique auto show, to kicking off the annual United Way giving campaign and the list could go on and on.

On one occasion I was invited to commemorate the satisfaction of a mortgage at a local congregation. The church was Pentecostal in practice and had a strong evangelistic approach. When I first arrived at the church I was struck by the décor and environment. There were musical instruments in the front of the church and visual aid projector to facilitate singing. All of this is foreign to me in a church setting. I grew up catholic and was an altar boy and a lecturer. My first memories of church were masses conducted in Latin. The services were very reverent and quiet. It wasn't until I was a college student that masses might include even a folk singer!

So, when the pop rock band started to play and the parishioners began to sing I knew I was experiencing something I had not seen before. After the first song the pastor started his sermon. He began by welcoming all that attended. "Brothers and sisters, we come here today to celebrate life. But to celebrate life we need to confess that we are not perfect and we have all sinned." He continued "brothers and sisters those who have sinned need to seek forgiveness from Jesus Christ. Brothers and sisters, I need those that have sinned to come to the front of this church and seek his forgiveness." As a group of parishioners came to the front of the church the others encouraged them and shouted out support. It was moving and exciting to see all the enthusiasm exhibited from the parishioners.

After confession the pastor announced that it was a special day for the church. In less than fifteen years the church mortgage had been paid off and that the mayor of our city was here to help recognize this accomplishment. He invited me to the podium. To be honest I was kind of caught up in all the enthusiasm, music and excitement. As I started my comments I shouted "Brothers and sisters I come here today to help you celebrate your great accomplishment. You should be proud of your accomplishment and we should all thank God for his support." As I continued to recognize my "brothers and sisters" who had been part of this effort I realized pretty quickly that I was not familiar with this type of worshiping and try to graciously get off the stage. To this day I still laugh at my effort to spread the gospel according to Dennis!

However, the mayor needs to represent the city in bad times as well. Nothing can be worse than losing a child in a tragic accident. Everyone in a community feels the loss and the mayor needs to give the community's condolences. I unfortunately had two such occasions and to this day think about those accidents. The first was a boy celebrating his thirteenth birthday with his friends and while walking back to his house for a party he was struck by a hit and run driver and died of his injuries. His classmates were devastated and the community was outraged at the callousness and cruelty of the driver. I was the first to arrive at the wake to give the community's condolences and when I approached the casket the young boy was dressed in his baseball uniform and holding his drum sticks. Being a father, heck just being a human being, my emotions filled my eyes with tears. You don't know the right words to use, but you tell the parents the whole community offers you their condolences.

The other tragic accident was high profile in that it involved three teenage girls who died in a car crash on Route 2 on their way back to the University of Massachusetts at Amherst where they attended school. Route 2 was notorious for being a dangerous winding and narrow road and accidents were not uncommon. The entire community was devastated by the loss. Family, friends, neighbors, former and current classmates all came to the wakes held at the same funeral home. The line stretched well outside the building. The tragic loss even brought out the cardinal who I greeted and introduced to the families. When I gave my condolences to the families I said, "If there is anything we can do for you please let me know." One of the mothers looked at me and said, "What we need is something you can't do for us." I am not sure what I would have said differently, but at the time I felt I was insincere by my comment and wondered how I could have been more supportive.

Another time I was reminded of the importance of the mayor was at another wake I attended. A woman had come to my office to interview me for her class project. I met with her and discussed the mayor's job and she left. A day or two later I noticed in the newspaper that her father had passed away. Historically mayors were known for attending wakes and funerals of constituents. While I attended wakes and funerals of people I knew I thought it would be perceived as political if I attended a ceremony and did not know the individual that had passed. Because I had just met this woman and she had been in the office I decided to stop in and give my condolences. The next day the woman appeared at my office and brought the condolence book that those who attended a wake would sign. I unfortunately had neglected to sign the book and she asked if I would be kind enough to sign it now. I signed it and realized that while I may have felt awkward about attending wakes and funerals of people I did not know my presences as mayor was important to them. In retrospect I think I may have made a mistake by avoiding those events.

Being mayor can be hard on family members when they encounter folks that are upset or disagree with one of your decisions or actions. These encounters can in turn upset your family. The *Eagle Tribune* regularly publishes a sound off column in the paper. The sound off column is unedited and allows anonymous readers to call in and provide their opinions on subjects of their choice. During one controversial clash with the unions a sound off comment was posted that compared me with Adolph Hitler. When my mother read the paper, and saw the comments she called me and was upset. "They said in the paper you were like Adolph Hitler!" I reminded her that I was a big boy and that I can take care of myself and sometimes people call you names when they disagree with you. I assured her that things would be alright and not to be upset. You always hope for civil discourse and debate but, unfortunately you cannot stop rude behavior.

There is a natural tendency to try to protect your family from any negative or awkward moments caused by your decisions or actions. Many times, you think about potential impacts and try to warn your family that people may say things to them that may be upsetting. During a labor dispute the police union was quoted in the paper, calling me "King" DiZoglio. I was concerned that my ten-year-old daughter, Sara, who went to school with children whose parents and relatives were police officers might be subjected to unkind comments from fellow students. I shared the newspaper article with her and asked her to read it so I could explain. After she read it she looked at me and said, "Dad if you are king does that make me a princess?" Needless to say, I gave her a big hug and said, "yes it does!"

But sometimes you cannot protect them. While at my office at city hall a constituent called my house and when my daughter answered the phone proceeded to yell at her because I had raised taxes. She told the woman that her dad was at the office and that I should call there to talk with me. I commended her on her response and told her that if that ever happened again she had my permission to hang up if she felt the person was being rude.

On the lighter side I remember when a constituent called the house during a snow storm and left a message asking me if I could get her street plowed. She explained that she was a nurse and was called into work but without the street plow clearing the road she would not be able to get to work. She had to leave a message because I was on vacation in Aruba and was not home. When I returned from my vacation and listened to my messages the next message was from the same woman saying the plow just got there and thanked me for getting the street plowed!

In this business you have an opportunity to meet "famous" people. "Famous" people are those who regularly appear in the media and can be recognized by the public. I have met all types of politicians, appointed officials and people ranging from mayors, to senators, to members of congress, to cabinet secretaries, religious leaders and entertainment celebrities. For the most part the encounters are formal and cordial. Occasionally these encounters can be amusing and memorable.

I remember when Mayor Buddy Cianci came to the region to talk about his work to revitalize the city of Providence, Rhode Island. Cianci was mayor of Providence from 1991 to 2002. He was one of the longest serving big city mayors and served for a total of twenty-one years during his career. He was known for his flamboyant style and for bringing a renaissance to the city. He is credited with bringing hotels and new housing to the city and establishing Providence as an arts and cultural center, uncovering the canal system in the city and organizing the WaterFire festival. He was also indicted in

2001 on federal extrusion and racketeering charges and served a five years sentence.

But, in 1998 he was known as a can-do mayor who brought vision and excitement to his city. The Merrimack Valley Chamber of Commerce invited him to come and talk with them about his approach and successes in an effort to give the City of Lawrence's new Mayor some "food for thought." The new mayor was unable to attend and since I was invited to the event as well, as the neighboring Mayor of Methuen, I was asked to sit with him through breakfast before his remarks. He was a colorful character and lived up to his flamboyant reputation. He arrived by helicopter and was accompanied by a Rhode Island State Police Officer. His uniform was ornate and the trooper looked like he was a Roman Carabinieri. Cianci wowed the crowd with stories and examples of Providence's successes. As the over six-foot-tall "Carabinieri" stood at attention behind Cianci the whole morning, I could not help but think of the robot from the movie *the Day the Earth Stood Still* brought to protect the alien.

Another amusing encounter involved, then-junior senator from Massachusetts, John Kerry. The senator was invited by Mayor Torigian to tour downtown Peabody and see firsthand how federal funds were being used to revitalize the downtown. I was asked to be part of the tour and served as a technical advisor to the mayor for any specifics involving funding or programming. The tour went well, and the senator learned how effective federal funding can be to help the communities he represented.

After giving his goodbye to the mayor the senator opened his car door to leave and noticed me waving goodbye some twenty feet away. He closed the door and walked toward me to personally say goodbye. I was honored that he decided to give me a personal goodbye, but I was not expecting it to be so memorable. I stood there waiting for the senator to reach me and when he arrived he stopped directly in front of me. However, he stood so close to me that I felt if I exhaled our noses would touch! I felt that my personal space was violated, but I thought it would be rude to pull back, so I held my position despite feeling uncomfortable. I am sure he felt the same way, and he also failed to pull back and adjust the distance between us. So, the future presidential candidate and secretary of state of the United States stood with me in downtown Peabody an inch apart wondering how the world was viewing our encounter! He graciously thanked me for the tour and the information and wished me good luck in my endeavors. He finally broke the tension and finished his goodbyes and turned around and left and ended our close encounter of the unusual kind.

Trying to improve the quality of life for the community is another role for the mayor. When I was first elected there was a group in the community that was trying to raise funds to create a youth center for Methuen. The group was dedicated and had some success in raising funds. After my election we held an inauguration ball and all the proceeds from the event went to this cause. After a number of years of fundraising, the group was significantly short of sufficient funds to start a project. Not only were there not enough funds to build a building, but the expertise of the group to actually run a facility was in question. Recognizing these shortfalls, I invited the president of the Merrimack Valley YMCA to meet with me and discuss our interest in a YMCA facility. Methuen did not have any YMCA facility. The Merrimack Valley YMCA had two facilities, one in Lawrence and one in Andover. It also had a summer camp in southern New Hampshire.

When I asked the YMCA president if there was any interest in having a facility in Methuen he enthusiastically said yes! I was initially excited by the prospect because the YMCA would be able to raise funds to construct a facility and would have the expertise to run the facility and we would finally get a youth center type facility for Methuen. I asked him when we could start the project. He told me "that's not how it works". He said, "First we develop the programming and determine the interest level in the kind of programs the YMCA runs. If successful we then conduct a capital campaign and construct a facility."

The YMCA program model used after school programs to gauge the interest level. I reached out to the school superintendent to discuss the idea. I was disappointed when the superintendent expressed some reservations. He was concerned about an outside entity using school facilities without school department supervision. Ultimately after a series of meetings the superintendent agreed to a pilot program at the Marsh School. The programming was a success and the YMCA expressed interest in moving to the next step. With the construction of the three new schools, older schools became surplus and the YMCA indicated it could renovate one of the schools into a YMCA facility. After I left office the YMCA was awarded one of the surplus schools and the city was able to secure a grant to help with the renovations. This grant along with the fund-raising efforts by the YMCA resulted in a YMCA facility in Methuen. After leaving office, I became Chairperson of the Methuen Branch YMCA Board of Directors and served on the Board until 2010 when I left due to term limits. Today there is talk of expanding the facility by adding a swimming pool to the programming.

After coming into office, I learned that the Presentation of Mary Academy that owned the former Edward Searles estate was selling artifacts to raise funds to sustain their high school and operations. Searles was a Methuen resident and at the turn of the 20th century and was worth $100M. He gained his wealth through marriage when he married Mary Hopkins, the widow of Mark Hopkins who built the Pacific railroad. Searles was enamored with his English heritage and a lover of fine arts and obtained many art treasures. He had suits of armor, tapestries, paintings, statues and other works of art. He constructed turrets and castle walls throughout the town and his properties. He built the town a high school and a grammar school. When he died he had no family and left his possessions to his man servant. The man servant also had no family so when he died he willed the possessions to the Catholic Church. The church used the Searles Estate for a catholic high school, Presentation of Mary Academy.

The artifacts being sold by the Academy were part of Methuen's history and needed to be secured for future generation of Methuen residents. I sent a letter to the Academy asking for a "first right of refusal" in all future offerings of artifacts. While I did not have any funds available to purchase any works of art, I thought I would be able to raise funds to keep these treasures in Methuen. I also learned during this time frame that the church had sold a statue of George Washington crossing the Delaware River. The work of art was commissioned by Searles and was made by Henry Vaughn. The church sold the sculpture to the Forest Lawn Cemetery in Glendale California. The sculpture is part of the Court of Freedom at the cemetery. Learning of this I contacted the officials at the cemetery and asked if they would be interested in selling the statue. Unfortunately, they indicated that the piece was not for sale. Preserving the history of a community is certainly a responsibility of a mayor.

The motivation for all of these efforts is to make your community special. If there is an opportunity to do something or make something special for the community, you need to try to make it happen. On Christmas day in 1991, the Gaunt Mill was destroyed by fire. The mill was located in the downtown on the banks of the Spicket River. When I came into office one of the priorities was to revitalize the downtown. One of the strategies we wanted to use was to enhance the public infrastructure and amenities in the downtown to encourage private investment. This vacant deteriorated site was an eye sore and detrimental to our efforts. The downtown needed more parking and open space and the site because of its location along the river could provide both of these needs.

In October of 1994, the city was able to get a State grant to help purchase the site and built a river walk park along the Spicket River, which included parking for the downtown. The park amenities included a pedestrian bridge across the river to connect the park, a gazebo for events, a tot lot, and an area that could be flooded in the winter for ice skating. The park was completed two year later and in October of 1996 a celebration to cut the ribbon to open the park was held.

A few months before the event was planned recording star and folk singer Livingston Taylor was performing to welcome Keith Lockhart as the new conductor for the Boston Pops. During the concert, which was televised, Taylor stated, "I like performing so much I would perform on a drain pipe in Methuen Massachusetts!" Learning of this comment I sent a letter to Livingston Taylor telling him that the people of Methuen have a good sense of humor and an even better place to hold a concert than on a drain pipe. I told him of the pending park opening and invited him to perform to help us celebrate. He accepted the invitation and performed to almost 1,000 Methuen residents. At the concert I thanked Taylor for coming and presented him with an engraved drain pipe with the words "Livingston Taylor Drain Pipe Tour, Methuen Massachusetts."

I was leaving office on January 2, 2000. The world was going to celebrate the turn of the millennium and I thought

Methuen should celebrate as well. The City of Boston had traditionally sponsored a "First Night" Celebration on New Year's Eve and it has been well received by Bostonians and the greater Boston community. As a community Methuen had never celebrated New Year's Eve but Y2K was coming. I approached one of Methuen's "doers" Rene Morissette, who was the Council on Aging Chairman. Morissette liked the idea and agreed to be the Chairman of the Methuen Celebration 2000 Millennium Committee. Along with his twenty-two committee members Morissette organized a gala celebration.

The event was a big success. The evening started with a "Gala Parade" though downtown. I was the Grand Marshall. There were five food venues and almost 25 entertainment venues ranging from Marionettes, magicians, clowns, jugglers, ice sculptures, and silent movies at the Methuen Music Hall, adult and middle school dances, skating, and a big band concert. The evening was capped off by a "light-up" ball drop at midnight and music synchronized fireworks.

Methuen was a special place on those days.

Chapter 12

"Quack, Quack, Quack"

There are only two communities in Massachusetts that have term limits for their chief elected officer, Lawrence and Methuen. When Lawrence changed its charter from the commission form to the current strong mayor form they instituted term limits for the mayor. The mayor can serve no more than two consecutive four-year terms. From 1950 to 1984 Lawrence elected John Buckley mayor for twenty-two of those thirty-four years. He was a dominate figure in Lawrence politics and many people wanted to prevent anyone from having that kind of dominance in the future so they included term limits in the charter change.

When Methuen changed their charter, they had just experienced the controversial appointment of Michael McLaughlin as town manager. As a suburb to Lawrence they too were concerned about a dominate person staying in office too long and included term limits in their charter. The mayor can serve no more than three consecutive two-year terms.

I was subject to the term limits approved by the voters. I always believed all elected officials have term limits in that an elected official must come back to the voters every election cycle and ask if they can stay for another term. You play by the rules and I knew I would be out of a job in six years if I was lucky enough to get re-elected twice. I was re-elected in 1995 by 84% of the vote. When I was re-elected to my third term in 1997 with 80% of the vote I officially became a lame duck. A lame duck, in politics, is an elected official who is approaching the end of their tenure. The official is often seen as having less influence with other politicians due to their limited time left in office. (27)

Not only was my time to serve limited but my effectiveness as a leader was limited as well. Being a lame duck affected my relationship with the city council, prevented consistent management prerogatives, and weakened my ability to represent the city with other levels of government.

My relationship with the city council deteriorated from the very beginning of my final term. It was started by an unusual policy decision. As stated earlier the revitalization of downtown was a major focal point over the course of the first four years in my administration. A redevelopment plan was initiated that led to a significant amount of public investment to spur on private investment. A downtown merchants association was established, and a land use strategy prepared by them recommended that restaurants could be a draw for the downtown. The strategy further recommended that the city market itself for that kind of use and support bringing restaurants to downtown.

The city was successful in attracting a restaurant with a good reputation to locate in the downtown. A building that was used as a function facility was leased to a restaurant call Renaldo's. During the permitting process the building lacked sufficient parking to meet the zoning requirements. Adjacent to the proposed site was a municipal parking lot that was rarely used. It was down a hill from the building and there were no other uses at the bottom of the hill that used the parking. The parking was created when an errant parcel was vacant and had little use but for parking. Keeping with the land use strategy I decided to make the parking available for the restaurant to meet the zoning requirements.

I learned quickly that the decision was going to become controversial. The proposed site was owned by a prominent family in the city. Mike Condon, who was a former city councilor, owned the building along with his wife and operated the function facility. Across the street from the building was a three-story building with an antiques store on the first floor and the second and third floors vacant and was owned by another prominent family in the city the Sheehan's. Robert Sheehan, the patriarch of the family made an appointment to see me after the decision was made. When he came in he said, "You know why I am here." I truly did not know why and said, "No, what's up?" He believed that the Condon's were being given special treatment and thought it was unfair. I explained my reasoning behind the decision and he responded, "what if I had a tenant for my building would you let me use the parking?" I answered in the affirmative, "Yes why not use the parking to help both you and Condon redevelop your buildings." Since Sheehan did not have any tenants lined up it was more of a rhetorical question but my answer did not change his opposition.

Since both families were prominent in the city they both had relationships with city councilors. City councilors began to take sides over the decision and began lobbying me. One of the ironies over the opposition to the decision was that the chair of the downtown association that oversaw the development of the land use strategy and marketing plan was Bob Sheehan the son of Robert Sheehan. Before the parking decision Sheehan was in full support of the recommendation to encourage restaurant use in downtown. This whole issue unfolded as a "Hatfield and McCoy" dispute. It seems that both families were upset with each other over a land acquisition deal where both parties felt that they were disrespected. The particulars did not matter, and the councilors did not care, they just lined up on either side.

As I tried to mediate this dispute the councilors became more entrenched with their positions. I was told that I would be gone next year, and my decision caused this split on the council.

As my influence began to slip away another added problem arose, the next mayoral election. Two of the sitting city councilors had announced they would be candidates for mayor. The majority of the councilors endorsed Councilor Larry Giordano and the split on the council got deeper. What exacerbated the situation further was that Giordano needed to separate himself from the other candidates and began to use the council to do so. He began to create issues to start defining his campaign.

The first disagreement was over the use of grant funds to pay for historic exhibits at the Tenney Gate House. The Tenney Gate house is the home of the Methuen Historic Society and acts as Methuen's historic museum. One of Giordano's opponents for mayor was Sharon Pollard, who was a sponsor of the Methuen Historic Society. Since they were grant funds and I had contract authority the exhibits were purchased and installed at the Gatehouse. The councilors complained that they rather use the grant funds to extend sewer to a neighborhood or repave streets than to create a Methuen Historic Museum. Not so transparent was a resolution by the council right after they cited their objections to the historic exhibits to construct a Persian Gulf War Monument, which was unanimously approved. I guess sewer expansion and repaving streets weren't important anymore!

In retaliation for the historic exhibit contract the city council stripped my contract authority, which was $50,000, and reduced it to $10,000. (28) Delaying the issuing of contracts interfered with the efficient operations of the city government. Council rules require that any resolution requires a first reading and then a second reading before approval. Having to wait for a city council meeting and then having to wait for another city council meeting before a vote would delay issuing a contract up to six weeks. That does not even include the procurement time associated with selecting a vendor. This is not very efficient for a responsive government.

The first casualty of this new rule did not take long. The city had leased space on a water tower for radio antennas. In exchange for the lease the vendor provided cash and an antenna for police and fire 911 dispatches. The council voted against the contract citing a need for a study to determine the health risk of having an antenna on the water tower that had been there for dozens of years. To avoid having the community without 911 services I had to extend the contract for six months until the council without a study voted to approve the contract.

With the success of the Renaldo's restaurant the other downtown restaurants began to thrive. People were having to wait an hour or an hour and a half to get into Renaldo's and the other restaurants like the 1859 House, Shadi's Restaurant and the Red Tavern restaurant started to get the overflow from those that did not want to wait that long for a table. The plan was working and when the Mar-Lin warehouse located in an old mill in the downtown sold their building for a 97-unit housing development, which created a built in cliental for the commercial enterprises in the downtown, I thought "don't you love when a plan comes together!" But it was not going to be that easy.

The project needed a special permit from the ZBA to allow for the housing in the downtown. I had appointed Bob Sheehan as chair of the ZBA a number of years earlier. Sheehan was a successful businessman and active on the Methuen Downtown Association and I thought his energy, expertise and interest in revitalizing downtown would be an asset to the ZBA and the city. After the Renaldo's issue his enthusiasm for the downtown revitalization waned and he opposed the conversion of the old mill into housing. Not only would the project bring 97 families downtown to live and shop it also removed a vacant, underutilized and derelict building from the downtown.

With opposition from the ZBA the project filed a 40B housing application, which I supported. The comprehensive zoning provision, which is known as 40B, is an anti-snob zoning provision that allows a project to override local zoning provided the project creates at least 20% affordable housing if a community as a whole has less than 10% affordable housing as defined by the Commonwealth. Methuen is below the 10% and the 40B/comprehensive zoning application can gain approval at the State Housing Appeals Board if it is locally denied. Under the 40B provision the ZBA approved the application with Sheehan voting no. Councilor Giordano was opposed to the affordable housing project and despite the fact that the project had been approved and was moving forward led an effort to place the project on a referendum petition. (29) The city council voted to include the referendum at the next municipal election. I vetoed the resolution, the only veto I issued in the six years as mayor. The veto was overridden by the city council. So, without a chance of overturning the 40B approval the city council had the citizens' vote either for or against the housing project. The project was rejected by the citizens, but moved forward anyway due to the 40B provision.

With the mayoral election in full swing to replace me the city council became more political than they had been over my first and second term. At the end of a fiscal year any funds not spent to satisfy the budget are considered surplus and are placed in the "Free Cash" category. Many communities use "Free Cash" as a reserve or to cover unforeseen expenditures, like snow removal costs that exceed budgeted amounts. Giordano proposed giving tax rebates to the citizens using the "Free Cash". (30) While this is instant gratification it is not sound fiscal policy. I much rather use the funds as a reserve to keep taxes from rising into the future. In addition, employee contracts for both the municipal side and the school side where being negotiated and depending on the negotiation funds were going to be needed to satisfy the contracts. This was another effort by Giordano to separate himself from the other candidates for mayor. A workshop was held to consider the proposal, but fortunately it was rejected for the reasons outlined.

Each year the mayor submits a fiscal year budget for the upcoming year for possible cuts and approval by the city council. During the budget deliberation the city auditor and the mayor provide an estimate of what the tax rate would be if the budget was approved. The city auditor estimate uses the state aid proposed by the governor and any new taxes due to new growth during the year and suggests a possible impact on the average property tax bill. These are always estimates since the state legislature has not approved the budget and the exact amount of local aid has not been determined and new growth is projected based on building permits taken and not actual development status.

The FY 2000 budget was approved by the city council in June of 1999 by a 5 to 4 vote. Once the state budget is approved and local aid is finalized and the exact growth in new tax revenue is known the city council can approve the tax rate to generate the revenue to satisfy the budget. In December of 1999 the city council rejected setting the tax rate by a 5 to 4 vote. The two councilors who ran for mayor voted no. The press reported that some of the councilors blamed the bad blood between the mayor and the council. One councilor described it as "this was a political kiss-off, if you would, from the council to the mayor." (31)

I came into office without a tax rate set and I left office without a tax rate set. Isn't politics grand?

I spent the entire six years in office trying to maintain management rights for the city. It was a tedious process and many times frustrating, but it was worth it. There were two management rights issues I felt strongly about that the unions sought to change every time we sat down to negotiate a contract.

The first was the 24-hour shift advocated by the firefighters union. The schedules for firefighters are established to get the best coverage for 24/7 service. Firefighter work two 10-hour days and then are off a day and then work two 14-hour nights. They work 48 hours for the week. They then get four days off and the cycle begins again. Because they get four days off over an eight-week period they average 42 hours per week.

The firefighters wanted to change to a 24-hour shift. This schedule calls for a firefighter to work 24 hours and then the firefighter is off 24 hours and then works another 24 hours. They then have five days off. They work 48 hours for the week and over an eight-week period average 42 hours per week like the other shift schedule.

Firefighters claim that the 24-hour shift gives them an opportunity to spend more time with their families and will save the community money in overtime since firefighters would use less sick time because of the longer recovery time with this 24-hour shift.

My first concern with the 24-hour shift is safety, both safety for the firefighter and safety for the citizens they serve. While it is expected that firefighters will sleep during their shift it is not guaranteed that the firefighter will be well rested to perform their duties. Imagine if the 24-hour shift was in place during the Malden Mills fire. The fire broke out around 5:30 PM which would have been approximately 10 hours into their 24-hour shift. They would not have had an opportunity to sleep and would be fighting one of the biggest fires they have ever worked. Their safety and the safety of the other firefighters could be in jeopardy. At the same time the public that is being served by the firefighter may not have the full capabilities of the firefighter due to fatigue. Even without a Malden Mill type fire the public could be at risk. The fire department mans the ambulance over the 24-hour period. The firefighters that are on the ambulance could be called into action over the entire 24 hours and may not be able to perform their duties without proper rest. According to an International Fire Chiefs Association report, fatigue can decrease a firefighter's alertness, increase response time and reduce strength. Alertness falls after 10-12 hours of work and during the nighttime. (32)

My second concern with the 24-hour shift is the suggestion that it would save money for the community in overtime since firefighters would use less sick time. If a firefighter calls in sick on the 24-hour shift their replacement would receive time and a half for the entire 24 hours. It will cost thirty-six hours of pay to fill in for a sick firefighter because of this differential. With the benefit of subsequent real overtime budget figures my concerns seem to be verified. In fiscal year 1999 the fire department overtime budget was $532,485. After the institution of the 24-hour shift the fire department overtime budget continued to increase. In 2000 it was $632,731, in 2001 it was $577,041 and in 2002 it was $649,439. Hardly the savings suggested by the union.

The new mayor authorized the 24-hour shift for the fire department in January 2000, in the first month I left.

The second management rights issue involved outside details for police officers. Many patrolmen earn overtime pay by performing traffic management details for local and state government departments as well as utilities. They perform these details at four-hour minimum increments. If you work a three-hour detail you are paid for four hours. If you work five hours you are paid for eight hours and so forth. This overtime can significantly increase the salary of a police officer.

Police officers wanted to perform outside security details at establishments that serve alcohol. The police union sees this as an opportunity for their members to earn additional funds and they point out that the detail is paid for by the private concern.

While it is true that it is not a direct cost to the community it does expose the community to a great deal of liability. If the officer is hurt while doing this private detail, which is not uncommon in establishments where alcohol is served, then the officer would become injured in the line of duty. The community would be responsible for paying their disability salary as well as filling in for the shifts the officer would miss due to the injury with time and a half overtime. The risk is just too great for the community to allow for these private details.

The new mayor authorized the outside details for the police department in January 2000, in the first month I left.

These concessions to the unions were done to gain support as the new mayor began her administration. I believe that you cannot buy the support of the unions, you can only rent it. The first time you say no to the unions the support you thought you gained will be gone.

One could argue that these management prerogatives could have been changed when a new mayor is sworn in regardless if there were term limits, which is true. But unions have the consistent leadership to continue to request these rights and the long term staying power to wait out the sitting mayor until there is a more receptive mayor. Plus, it is still difficult to watch as items you fought for six years to prevent are granted as soon as you leave office.

Another limitation to my authority was the impact on my relationship with some officials outside of Methuen. It is logical that Methuen city councilors, municipal employees, unions and citizens would perceive me as a "lame duck" but when it influenced my responsibility to represent the city with officials outside of Methuen, it surprised me.

Behind city hall was a 24-acre parcel once owned by Charles Tenney, one of three philanthropists who lived and greatly influenced the development of Methuen. The parcel once housed Greycourt the palatial home of Tenney. Greycourt was destroyed by fire but the foundation and the history of the estate was still important to Methuen. The Tenney Castle Gatehouse, Methuen's historic museum, is located at the entrance way to the parcel. The Commonwealth acquired the parcel, and it became a Massachusetts state park, and is a satellite of the Lawrence Heritage State Park.

The park was under construction and would soon be open and the State Department of Environmental Management (DEM), which ultimately became the Department of Conservation and Recreation, would manage the park and an agreement between the city and DEM needed to be negotiated to spell out the responsibilities of the city and the state in managing and maintaining the park. Negotiations began during my last year in office. With almost eight months left in my term the DEM negotiator suggested that we stop negotiating and wait for the new mayor to complete the negotiations. I was surprised by her recommendation. While there were some details still to work out I did not perceive them to be insurmountable. I rejected her suggestion and demanded we conclude our negotiations. The process became slower but we were able to complete the deal.

When I ran for mayor I knew that there were term limits and if successfully re-elected I would be there for only six years. In some ways it was a gracious way to leave. Not overstaying your welcome. No hand on your back telling you to leave. But I do feel that I was not as effective as I was during the first four years and wonder if we would have accomplished more if the term limits did not limit my effectiveness.

Term limits in Methuen will continue for the foreseeable future. In 2011 the Methuen Charter Change Commission presented to the voters a proposed change that would eliminate term limits. The charter change was defeated soundly 6,203 to 2,004. It will be a long time before anyone considers eliminating term limits for Methuen.

Chapter 13

"It Was The Best Job I Ever Had"

When people ask me what is was like being mayor I respond by saying, "It was the best job I ever had". For a person who got into this business to make a difference you could not ask for a more challenging position than mayor. Every day and I mean every day you had an opportunity to either help a citizen with a problem or do something that made the community better. The job requires you to be a problem solver and navigate through the government bureaucracies, the politics that drive decisions, and the people who resist change because of the fear of the unknown.

You make a difference by making government work to achieve your goals and objectives. This is not as easy as it sounds. Resistance comes from many quarters; city councilors, municipal employees and citizens but you can be successful.

One of the priorities I had when elected was to encourage economic development in the community. The City of Methuen traditionally has an unemployment rate which exceeds the state average. The jobs that would be created through economic development would help address this issue. In addition, the property and personal taxes generated by economic development would help keep Methuen affordable. One of the draws to live in Methuen is its affordability and a reasonable tax rate would go a long way to keeping taxes down but still provide good municipal services.

As mentioned earlier the turnaround of Malden Mills after the fire was certainly a success. A larger, modern facility was constructed after the fire, and additional jobs were created due to the notoriety and goodwill generated by Malden Mills' decision to rebuild. More tax revenue was generated, and the water and sewer use continued, and it generated funds to upgrade the water and sewer infrastructure.

The downtown was experiencing a revival. Besides the park mentioned earlier a new iconic clock tower was constructed using grant funds. New restaurants located downtown along with a bakery. The merchants organized and a "main street" program was started to promote the downtown with various events and marketing techniques.

Efforts to further grow the tax base of Methuen required a proactive approach to economic development. Attracting new businesses to the community is always a good thing. But, more growth actually occurs if you can help existing companies upgrade and expand. My economic development team identified businesses that were doing well and Gene O'Neil, my Economic Development Director, arranged for me to visit these companies and learn more about their plans and needs.

During a visit to Parlex a manufacturer of flexible circuit boards, we found that the business had grown so fast that a large portion of the business was operating out of portable trailers. We encouraged the president of the company to expand the building and modernize their operations. The president indicated that the company was interested in improving their image and stature in the growing market and I suggested that if he went forward with an expansion that we could arrange for the entrance way into the facility to be considered a street and the address to the new building would be One Parlex Way. He liked the idea and we arranged for help from the quasi-public state business finance agency, MassDevelopment, to finance a 38,000 square foot expansion. The expansion at One Parlex Way created 75 new jobs.

We had similar success with a company called Micro Touch, a touch screen computer manufacturer, located in the Griffin Brook Industrial Park. During our visit with the president of the company we learned that the company would benefit with the availability of natural gas to the industrial park. We worked with the gas utility and identified other businesses that would benefit from the natural gas in the park and convinced them to extend the gas line to the park. Micro Touch expanded their building by 60,000 square feet and would add 400 new jobs. Another company in the Griffin Brook Industrial Park that took advantage of the new gas line was ULVAC, a maker of semi-conductor assembly equipment. ULVAC constructed a 40,000 square foot expansion.

One of the most interesting efforts to encourage economic development involved the revitalization of the Methuen Mall property. At one time the mall was one of the premier shopping malls in Massachusetts. A 500,000 square foot mall that housed retailers like Sears, Jordan Marsh, Filene's and

Ann & Hope. The mall was owned by Met Life and their tenants Sears and Jordan Marsh, which was later acquired by Macy's, expressed interest in having Met Life construct a second story to the mall for their use to expand their presence in Methuen. Met Life declined their request and New England Development built the Rockingham Mall in Salem New Hampshire just seven miles away to meet the retailers' needs and they both left the Methuen Mall.

When I arrived in 1994, the mall was struggling to keep tenants. The anchors had left the mall and the synergy between the retailers for consumers to do comparison shopping was gone. Efforts to encourage more traffic to the mall included adding a Registry of Motor Vehicle branch and a new restaurant but they did very little to reverse the slide. City Councilor Giordano suggested more could be done to reverse this trend and that I should establish a task force to deal with the issue.

It was clear to me that Met Life was not sufficiently engaged in the process to revitalize the mall and that a task force would have very little impact on bringing meaningful change to the mall. However, I established the task force anyway and appointed Giordano to be on the task force. It is harder to criticize when you are on the task force established to solve the problem.

When establishing the task force, I was interviewed by the *Eagle Tribune* and during the interview I declared that Met Life was an absentee landlord and they were not serious about turning the mall around. I further suggested that people who bought Met Life Insurance were condoning the company's actions. The day after I was quoted in the paper criticizing Met Life I got a call from the company representatives in New York City asking for a meeting. The meeting was slightly confrontational in that I needed to push Met Life to commit to the revitalization of the mall. In the response to the push they expressed an interest in selling the property. The task before us was to find someone to buy the property and turn it around.

Although there was no "for sale" sign up we began to tell developers that the property was for sale. One of the developers contacted was Marty Spagat from Minuteman Development who successfully developed office/R&D buildings in the Andover Industrial Park. Spagat was the developer interested in developing similar use properties in Methuen earlier and was deterred by neighborhood opposition. Spagat and his investors proposed building a number of office/R&D buildings on the Methuen Mall site. While the development was a significant departure from the current use the upside was great. The development would create good paying professional jobs for Methuen and significant tax revenue.

Spagat acquired the property, but before the project could move forward the market for Office/R&D space dried up. Searching for another use Spagat proposed a lifestyle entertainment center. The anchor of the development would be a twenty screen movie theater, with five restaurants and supportive retail. At the time entertainment theme shopping centers were new to the industry and the Loop as it was to be called would be the first in New England with this new approach. The site was perfect for this use since it was off Route 213 and connected to I-93 and I-495 the premier interstate highways in the region. Although sufficient infrastructure was available at the former mall site we obtained a Public Works Economic Development (PWED) grant from the Commonwealth to repave the streets surrounding the site and add suitable traffic management controls.

Since this was a new concept for New England the developers had to obtain financing outside of the region. They approached Lehmann Brothers out of New York to finance the project. As part of their due diligence Lehmann Brothers asked to meet with city officials. Their intent was to gauge the community's interest and commitment to the project. I invited their representative to a meeting in my office where we orchestrated a presentation. As part of the presentation I provided an overview of the community and listed the investments the community was making in the schools, library, public safety and recreational facilities. The city auditor then assured them that the community had financed all of these investments without a Proposition 2 ½ override and that the city was below the Proposition 2 ½ tax levy limit. The city engineer then provided a timeline to complete the PWED funded infrastructure upgrades showing that they would be completed before the completion of the center. The building inspector informed them that we had just completed the construction of the new Malden Mills' facility on schedule and that the inspector that was brought on to ensure inspections were timely would be assigned to their project. Lehmann Brothers decided to finance the project.

Despite securing a $50M reuse of the Methuen Mall and tripling the tax revenue of the property to $1M Councilor Giordano, who announced his candidacy for mayor to replace me, criticized the project for prioritizing road improvements to support the project as opposed to repaving streets throughout the community. He specifically mentioned an intersection on the edge of the development that was not included in the improvement program as an example. The road improvements for the "Loop" were being paid for with a State PWED grant and could only be used to support an economic development project that created jobs and new tax revenue. Because of Giordano's concerns we reached out to the state and were able to secure an amendment to the grant and additional funds to include the intersection recommended were awarded. (33)

With the Loop as an attraction the Pleasant Valley Street corridor saw additional development. Wal-Mart, Target and Home Depot opened stores and a new restaurant was constructed and two older restaurants renovated. In addition, Mann's Apple Orchard, the longest family owned business in Methuen built a new retail building.

Before coming to Methuen my career focused on community and economic development so bringing this expertise to the mayor's job was a natural. Besides focusing on economic development, I also saw an opportunity to focus on neighborhood revitalization. The Arlington neighborhood in Methuen abutted the City of Lawrence. It mirrored the kind of housing stock prevalent in Lawrence, two and three family houses with very little homeownership. In fact, the homeownership rate in the Arlington neighborhood was 30% homeowners and 70% absentee landlords. Methuen as a whole was the exact opposite with 70% homeowners and 30% absentee landlords. When in Peabody, I had developed a first-time homeownership program that provided grant funds to income eligible families to help them with a down payment to buy a home. It was a deferred payment loan that provided a portion of the down payment and when the homeowner sold the home they would pay back the loan with the sale proceeds and the repayment could be used for another first-time buyer. To improve the homeownership in the Arlington neighborhood I proposed using this tool.

Since the Arlington neighborhood was different from the other neighborhoods in Methuen it was somewhat neglected by the city. The city applied for grants to help revitalize the neighborhood, but it was a top down kind of program with the city telling the neighborhood what they needed. One neighbor who resisted this approach was Linda Soucy. She sensed the city was not responsive to the neighborhood needs and decided to organize the neighborhood to control its own destiny.

When prostitution was rampant in the neighborhood she complained to the police, but the response was the police coming down and moving the activity to another street still leaving the problem. So, she took to the streets with video cameras recording Johns approaching women. The attention she brought to those people engaged in this activity literally drove them out of the neighborhood. Her success was recognized both inside Methuen and outside by the Boston media. She became the leader of the neighborhood and when I approached her about the first-time homebuyers program she told me that the neighborhood was not interested. I think she perceived it as another top down program telling the neighborhood what they needed.

I told her I was disappointed that they were not interested, but asked if she could help me by looking over the program and giving me her feedback. I told her I was going to try to offer the program to other neighborhoods and wanted to design a program that people would use. After she reviewed the specifics of how the program would work she suggested some changes. The changes were good and I thanked her for her help and told her I would change the program to reflect her recommendations. She was surprised at my willingness to make the changes and told me that if we did make the changes the neighborhood would be interested in participating.

The results of this discussion led to a strong and productive partnership with the neighborhood. With this new line of communication, we learned that the neighborhood's image was adversely affected by graffiti. A quick walk through the neighborhood verified this concern. Armed with rollers and brushes I met up with neighborhood volunteers and we painted out all the graffiti we could find. Working with the city council we passed an ordinance requiring landlords to remove graffiti on their property within thirty days or be subject to a fine to maintain the progress we initially made. We left sufficient paint for the neighborhood to police the public spaces since graffiti continued to appear.

The problem needed a continual effort to eradicate graffiti from the neighborhood. One example that illustrates this need was a hand ball court in the neighborhood park. Graffiti was initially painted over, but it did not take long for graffiti to appear again. The neighborhood volunteers painted it over again and the cycle continued for a number of weeks. The graffiti was associated with neighborhood gangs marking their territory. The graffiti got smaller and smaller in an attempt to deter the neighbors from painting it out. The neighbors did not waiver and in response painted the hand ball court a dark blue which prevented the well-used court from being used since you cannot see the ball coming off the wall. The neighbors agreed to repaint the wall white for hand ball use if the youth discontinued posting the graffiti. A deal was struck and the neighborhood became graffiti free.

The neighbors wanted to deal with the gangs that were active in the neighborhood and felt getting the children engaged early with education and social programs would help. They formed the Methuen Arlington Neighborhood Corporation (MAN, Inc.) to run the social service programs. The city made an old sewer pump station that was not needed and abandoned available for delivering the programs. We obtained grant funding to renovate the building and ultimately a new building was constructed to provide a number of educational and social programs for the neighborhood.

The city regularly filed a Community Development Block Grant (CDBG) application and the uses of the funds were driven with neighborhood input. The streets and sidewalks were repaired, the neighborhood park was improved, drainage and sewer upgraded and signs were added to identify that you were entering Methuen. This greatly improved the image of the neighborhood.

The first-time homebuyers program was beginning to work, but it was slow in turning the homeownership rate around. The neighborhood identified the worst street for homeownership and condition and decided to create a "model block" program to turn that street around. Tenney Street was the targeted neighborhood and resources were focused on the street.

I established a Building Safety Task Force to identify vacant and abandoned buildings throughout the community with the intent of using the powers of the city to approach owners to demand they improve the property or sell it to the city for redevelopment. I chaired the task force and invited the police and fire chiefs, city solicitor, building inspector, health inspector, DPW and Linda Soucy, since many of the abandoned properties were in the Arlington neighborhood to participate. The task force created a top ten list of properties and published the list in the newspaper. The task force invited property owners to meet with them and the task force was very successful at getting these properties repaired and occupied. One of the first properties we focused on was on Tenney Street.

Tenney Street was repaved and a neck down installed to reduce speed and improve pedestrian safety on the Street. MAN Inc. social service facility was constructed next to the park that was upgraded. The city assembled four housing lots where the homes were either destroyed by fire or obtained for back taxes and made a deal with Habitat for Humanity to construct four homes for first time homebuyer. Within a relative short period of time the homeownership rate increased to 70%. The mantra became "if you can do it on the worst street in the neighborhood you can do it everywhere."

The last piece of the effort was to improve public safety in the Arlington Neighborhood. The community policing program, which the city created, focused its initial attention on the Arlington Neighborhood. Street lights were added to discourage inappropriate activities. Police officers walked beats and met with neighbors. The neighborhood came a long way in those six years.

A foundation for good municipal services is to have up to date facilities that can meet the needs of the community. During the campaign I regularly heard from parents concerned about the class sizes at the Methuen schools. When I came into office Superintendent Littlefield expressed concern over limited classroom space and the impact on class sizes. The CGS school that was built just before I came into office was built to house 1,200 students but had an enrolment of 1,600. There was significant single-family housing growth in the community and there was concern that this trend would continue to add students to the overcrowded classrooms.

Littlefield suggested we conduct an enrollment analysis to predict future classroom needs. To encourage me to consider this analysis he offered to pay half for the analysis. If we were serious about building more space this was definitely part of the due diligence and his incentive was not needed, but I did take him up on his offer. If we were going to do this we needed a strong partnership to move forward.

The demographic analysis came back with a prediction that school enrollment would increase by 1,200 students over the next ten years. What surprised me most by the analysis was that the growth was not coming from the hundreds of new single-family houses being built but from the older housing stock. Older families were selling their homes to downsize or due to retirement and new families where buying their homes as starter homes and their families were just beginning to grow. The new single-family homes had higher price tags because of the new construction and new owner families were already in the school system or enrolled in private schools.

To meet the needs, it was suggested that we expand three schools in the community: Marsh, Tenney and the Timony.

Funding this aggressive building program would be a challenge but Methuen was fortunate in that the Hispanic population was growing rapidly and the Commonwealth had decided to help communities desegregate their school systems by providing funding incentives. Communities that tied their building programs to desegregation would qualify for 90% funding. Methuen had 553 Hispanic students in 1980 and that number grew to 2,012 by 1990.

While Methuen was fortunate to have potential access to extra state assistance, desegregation itself was not without its controversy. To address desegregation a desegregation plan needed to be developed. New school district lines needed to be drawn to assign an equal number of minority students to each school. Once the plan was designed public hearings were held to explain the proposed new district lines and to take public comment. Changing which school a student currently attended was controversial. Many parents felt the neighborhood school concept was being phased out and their children were being relocated to other neighborhoods. The plan tried to minimize this impact but displacement did occur.

As chair of the school committee I facilitated the public hearings. During one of the hearings a woman approached the podium and criticized the plan. She concluded her comments by asked "where are all these children coming from?" A number of people perceived that the increase in Hispanic students was caused by children enrolling from neighboring Lawrence. At the time Lawrence's Hispanic population exceeded fifty percent and many believed Lawrence parents were sending their children to Methuen public schools. Because of this perception the school department established rigorous residency verification standards. Two forms of residence verification were required to register your child and a verification officer was hired to monitor pick up and drop off activity and investigate any complaints that might be filed. The school department was confident that the vast majority of the students were residents. So, when the woman asked her questioned I leaned forward into the microphone and said "Methuen". The response resulted in many in attendance looking at each other and shrugging their shoulders in agreement.

While the numbers were in our favor that 90% funding would be available, the funding process required that Methuen produce the design for the schools so that an application to the Commonwealth's School Building Assistance Bureau (SBAB) could be filed. The cost for the design was $4M. It was a gamble, but one I felt was worth doing. I thought the worst case scenario would be that one of the schools would be funded and we could use the other designs for future applications. The total cost of the project was $70M for all three schools. The project would not require a Proposition 2 ½ override since the city would be responsible for only 10% of the project cost. The city's share of the project, $7M, would add less than $10 a year to the average homeowners' tax burden, less than $1 a month.

As you can imagine the parents with school age children were in support of the project. However, we needed to make sure that the elderly residents on fixed incomes and without school age children were on board. I reached out to the elderly community through the senior center and other venues and built support for the project. In February of 1995, I approached the city council regarding the borrowing along with 150 Methuen residents. Believe it or not the council ended up debating whether I would be allowed to speak. Three councilors felt the meeting was for private citizens to speak to them about the project not the mayor. This was a continuation of the debate over the responsibilities of the mayor and the city council that we had a year earlier when I was first elected. Five councilors agreed to let me speak but council rules required six votes to waive the rules and I was denied an opportunity to present the project. Citizens came to the podium and asked questions. I had the answers, but was denied an opportunity to address those questions. After wasting three quarters of an hour the council allowed me to share my thoughts. The council approved the bond authorization.

The SBAB approved our application for all three schools. That was the good news; the bad news was that we now needed to build all the schools relatively at the same time. We were able to start the Marsh school first since there was more new construction and the designs were easier to complete. The Timony was next and the Tenney last but within a few months of each other. Since the last two schools had more renovation and less new construction there was a feeling that the existing furniture and equipment could be reused. There was significant lobbying by parents to purchase all new equipment and furniture under the argument of equity. Since all the k thru 8 schools in the system would now be built within a four-year period it did make some sense that all the schools have no educational inequities. This would also help in future redistricting that would occur to ensure all the schools had equal numbers of minority students. To accomplish this $6M more in funding would be needed. With the same coalition of supporters, I approached the city council and the additional funds were authorized.

The Nevins Memorial Library was built in 1883 by the Nevins family in honor of David Nevins Sr. It has served as Methuen's library ever since. The Nevins Library was not a municipal facility. It was operated by the Nevins Library Board of Trustees and it used an endowment set up by the Nevins family to run the library. The endowment was insufficient to support the library and the Methuen provided some funds to maintain the library.

In 1883, the population of Methuen was approximately 4,500 people and in 1995 it was 42,000 people. The Nevins Library had no elevator, no sprinkler system, and no HVAC system, was not handicap assessable and did not meet the needs of the city. The library trustees approached me about helping them modernize the facility while preserving the architectural character. It was a much-needed project and there were state library renovation grant funds available to offset some of the costs to do so. We hired Adrian Tappe and Associates to conduct a feasibility study for $25K. The building program called for a doubling of the size of the library and adding to their book collection. This $7M project expanded the library and stayed true to the historic character of the existing building, added an elevator, handicap accessibility, and a new HVAC system. We were able to obtain a $2M State Public Library Construction Grant to offset the cost of the project. But since it was not publicly owned Methuen was not able to bond for the renovations.

The trustees did not want to give up control of the facility, but desperately wanted to renovate the library. I recommended we create a library board of commissioners; the membership would mirror the board of trustees. The library would be managed by this new municipal library commission and the facility would become a municipal facility until the bond was paid off. Once the note was paid off the Library Board of Commissioners would be eliminated and the Board of Trustees would regain control. It was a delicate negotiation between the trustees and the city council over the control issue, but we were able to convince both parties that this approach would accomplish everyone's goals.

The library was not the only facility the Nevins family provided for Methuen. The family also constructed the Nevins Home for the Aged. As with the library a portion of the Nevins Home was in disrepair and with insufficient funds available to restore the building it was scheduled to be demolished. With a piece of Methuen's history in danger we sought out a federal grant to construct affordable housing and were able to secure a $3.4M HUD grant to renovate the building for forty assisted living units for the elderly to add to the existing Nevins Home housing and programming.

The Nevins Library and Home were not the only historic structures that were in disrepair. The Central Fire Station was built at the turn of the twentieth century. The roof and parapet needed repair and the bricks needed to be cleaned and re-pointed and the covings and trim needed to be repainted and preserved. We obtained a historic renovation grant from the Massachusetts Historical Commission and upgraded the facility for $1.5M.

The impact of the growing number of school aged children did not just affect the schools it also had an impact on the youth sports programs throughout the community. There were now thousands of Methuen children playing sports and the demand for playing fields had grown. With little space to build new fields we decided by lighting fields across the community we could increase the availability of existing fields to meet the demand. With the support of the youth sporting groups I approached the city council regarding floating a bond for $2.1M to add lighting to a number of fields, reconstruct the tennis courts at the high school, improve soccer fields, field hockey fields, baseball and softball fields and the Pop Warner and practice football fields.

The last investment area we tried to tackle was road improvements. With the aggressive investment strategy described underway there were little bond funding available to focus on road repairs. We needed to be smart and creative to begin chipping away at the road improvement needs. To define our need I commissioned a pavement management survey and program. The survey found that 60% of the roads in the city needed to be repaved. Included in the programming portion of the study was a computer model program that would suggest various investment strategies by street condition and available funding. It was an effort to get more scientific as to which streets would be prioritized and less political in the decision making. What we also discovered during the analysis was that many of the streets needed drainage improvements and if the improvement were not done the repaving would not last very long. I did not want our improvement program to be only a cosmetic improvement program and opted to include drainage into our prioritization process. The city was getting a lot of pressure to separate the storm sewer from the sanitary sewer from the EPA. Historically communities combined their drainage and sewer systems before the EPA expressed environmental concern over the combined systems. Older communities like Methuen and Lawrence had more combined systems. Treating storm water as sewerage is costly. By eliminating drainage from the sewer system, the city would save money on sewer treatment.

Connecting the two needs was logical in that the condition of the streets were poor because of the drainage problem. And the drainage problems were exasperated by the combined sewer systems. Using sewer enterprise funds to separate the systems brought a new funding source to the problem and helped the city improve the road conditions, the drainage problems and reduce sewer treatment costs. Using Chapter 90 Funds, State funds allocated for road repair and sewer enterprise funds we were able to invest $5M in road improvements. We also constructed or repaired sidewalks around the school building projects to encourage student to walk to school and provide a safe way to do so.

In order to be able to afford all these improvements the city needed to be financially sound. The city administration had to be efficient and cost savings needed to be identified. We restructured our health care program for municipal employees. We added a Blue Cross Blue Shield HMO product advocated for by the unions but kept the premiums the same to avoid incentivizing the migration of healthy enrollees from the indemnity product to the HMO. Methuen is self-insured for health care costs and is responsible for actual costs to provide the care. To protect it from unforeseen costs it obtains "stop loss" insurance. We rebid this policy and saved over $200,000. We privatized the trash collection and transitioned from a main frame computer system to a multi-server system, all of which saved the city money.

Because of these and other savings we were able to keep the average tax bill increases over the six years in office to an average of $22/year. In fiscal year 1997 we were able to actually reduce the average tax bill by $6. Because of this fiscal conservatism Methuen saw its excess levy capacity under Proposition 2 ½ increase significantly. Excess levy capacity is the difference between what a community levies in taxes and the levy ceiling allowed under Proposition 2 ½. (34) When I came into office in 1994, Methuen had a Proposition 2 ½ excess levy capacity of $8,000, when I left in 1999 the levy capacity was $4M. What this indicator means is that residents were taxed less than what is allowed under Proposition 2 ½. This provides a savings to them and it gives the municipality more room to tax in the future if the community needs additional funds to support capital projects or significant budget increases. It also greatly reduces the need for a future Proposition 2 ½ override.

Another fiscal indicator is tax stabilization funds. A tax stabilization fund allows a community to set aside unencumbered funds for future needs. Communities can use this type of reserve account to save money for a "rainy day", manage debt service, think long term and build resident confidence in government. When I came into office the tax stabilization fund balance was $2,500 when I left office it was $2M. A significant portion of this increase came from our ability to earn arbitrage on our borrowing for the school buildings. We were able to borrow the funds needed to pay the school contractors in the future at tax exempt rates and invested in short term notes and earn a profit since the investment paid a higher return than the cost to borrow the money.

The bond rating agencies rewarded the city by giving the community a Municipal Investment Grade (MIG) 1 for short-term notes and a long-term bond rating of A-1. These bond ratings measure the credit worthiness of a municipality and affect the ultimate interest rates the community will pay when borrowing funds through a bond. I had hoped for a higher long-term bond rating and pointed out to the rating companies the community's excess levy capacity. I felt it was a significant factor to ensure sufficient funds where available to satisfy any future notes, but the rating agencies felt the community should collect that excess capacity and put it into a tax stabilization fund. This option would be difficult politically and they denied my request for a bond rating increase. Recently the city was able to dedicate their restaurant sales tax increase to the tax stabilization fund and the rating agencies increased the city's bond rating.

Although I clearly focused on Methuen there is always a need to think regionally. Methuen participates in a number of regional initiatives and it is important to truly participate in the management of these initiatives. The city participates in a regional sewer treatment facility, Greater Lawrence Sanitary District (GLSD). The GLSD membership is comprised of Methuen, Lawrence, Andover, North Andover and Salem N.H. The GLSD processes 52M gallons of wastewater per day from the region. Methuen's assessment is over $2M a year, but it is more than the money that requires active participation.

During my administration Lawrence proposed privatizing the GLSD facility. The Mayor of Lawrence wanted to sell the plant to a private concern and use the upfront revenue to address the combined sewer overflow problems for the city. EPA had issued a consent order and wanted Lawrence to begin separating their sanitary and drainage sewer system. Lawrence is the biggest user of the GLSD and would receive the biggest share of any sale. While Methuen is second to Lawrence I thought the resulting impact of the sale outweighed any short-term benefit. Therefore, I was opposed to the proposal since the communities would lose control over future assessments and management of the facility.

In addition, the GLSD was debating on how to deal with the sludge, which is the byproduct of the treatment. Today the sludge is converted into methane gas through a digester, but in 1999 it was proposed to convert the sludge into pellets and use the material for fertilizer. Both these proposals needed communities to participate and send qualified people to represent them at the board of commissioners. Methuen had two appointments and I appointed an accountant and an engineer to represent Methuen's position on these important issues.

The Merrimack Valley Transit Authority (MVRTA) provides transit to the region and Methuen is one of the 15 member-communities. While I was mayor I chaired the advisory committee that oversees the MVRTA administration. The MVRTA provides fixed route bus service, commuter bus service to Boston, and EZ Trans service. EZ Trans service is ADA and non- ADA assistance for senior citizens 60 years old or greater.

While I was Mayor I received a number of complaints from the elderly residents regarding the EZ Trans service. The MVRTA used three vendors to provide the EZ Trans service.

The complaints were targeted to one of the vendors. As chair of the advisory committee I invited the MVRTA Administrator to a series of meetings with the representatives from the senior center where the complaints originated. Ultimately, we were able to intervene on the riders' behalf and negotiated a change of the vendor for Methuen.

In 1997, the Commonwealth of Massachusetts eliminated some of the counties in the state. Methuen is part of Essex County, which is one of those that were eliminated. Before it was eliminated I represented Methuen at the Essex County Advisory Board. I was also appointed to the executive committee and played a leadership role in defining a role for county government.

County government had lost a meaningful role in providing services. It was led by three elected county commissioners and the services provided by the county were sometimes duplicative of municipal services or had no useful purpose. The advisory board attempted to bring some relevance to the organization of communities brought together by county boundaries and statute.

The advisory board formed a collaborative purchasing program, where communities purchased material and supplies collectively to save money. It also tried to promote the historic character throughout the county with its support of the Essex National Heritage Commission. Essex Heritage is a non-profit organization that works with communities in Essex County to save the unique historic, cultural, and natural places character of Essex County. The region was designated as a National Heritage Area by an act of Congress in 1996.

When Essex County government was eliminated the opportunity for the communities to continue looking at ways to work together and regionalize efforts was lacking. I approached the executive director of the Merrimack Valley Planning Commission (MVPC), which I would lead someday, to consider expanding the commission's role to include more regionalization activities. While MVPC had only 15 members from Essex County it did include Methuen and its surrounding neighbors. MVPC was focused more on traditional planning activities like land use, transportation, economic development and environmental preservation. The executive director was not interested in expanding the role of the agency despite the fact that the mission statement for MVPC when it was established in 1959 was to promote cooperation and coordination in the region. When I was appointed the executive director in 2007 one of my first efforts was to establish the Merrimack Valley Mayors and Managers Coalition, which led to a series of successful regional efforts in areas such as regional purchasing, renewable energy and conservation, and shared services.

Being actively involved in regional initiatives can make a difference in the services you receive from that entity.

I think we were able to accomplish a great deal during my six years in office, but I wonder today if we would be able to have the same successes in today's environment. It has been said that the art of politics is compromise. As a political scientist I lived by this mantra my entire career. I always felt that I rather have some progress than no progress and always approached a policy decision with an open mind with the willingness to compromise. A compromise allows policies to move forward and prevents government inaction. While government inaction can be a viable public policy decision many time the desire to initiate a policy is to address a problem. If we can agree a problem exists, then compromises to address the problem make sense.

Today politicians do not favor this approach. A new word "consensus" has replaced "compromise". To the politician today "consensus" means if I agree with your position I will support the decision, otherwise I will not support the suggest policy decision. However, there is no willingness to compromise so both parties can support the suggested policy decision. This attitude creates government gridlock. It prevents the government from making needed decisions and makes the government non- responsive to the citizens it serves. This leads to citizens having unfavorable opinions of government. They lack confidence in the government and look for outsiders who offer unrealistic solutions or viable plan to move public policy forward. Politicians need to be honest with citizens and offer realistic solutions based on transparent discussions around facts and options.

When I left office in January of 2000 I produced my last *Methuen on the Move* local cable show. During the show I warned residents about the demagogues in our community. They will tell you everything that is wrong about the community and not suggest how you can make it better. Their immediate reaction to any suggestion is "no". Their mistrust limits our ability to move ideas forward. I am concerned that the ability to do big things is gone. With social media today, falsehoods are easily put forth as gospel with no ability to provide a counterpoint. Ideas are not the enemy and if you cannot talk about them without accusations of mistrust and negativity then we certainly can't make a difference.

Notes

1. Stockdale was a candidate for Vice President of the United States in the 1992 presidential election, on Ross Perot's independent ticket. During the Vice Presidential debate he uttered these famous words to attempt to introduce himself to the American People. From Wikipedia
2. *Merrimack Valley Priority Growth Strategy*, Merrimack Valley Planning Commission, 2015. MVPC.org
3. Commission Form of Government. This form of government originated in Galveston, Texas as a response to the Galveston Hurricane of 1900, mainly for the reason that extra support was needed in certain areas. After its constitutionality was tested and confirmed, this form of government quickly became popular across the state of Texas and spread to other parts of the United States. From Wikipedia
4. Senator Paul Tsongas from Massachusetts and former Presidential candidate speaking about McLaughlin in 1990, Paul Tsongas was quoted, "In all my life in politics, from the Lowell City Council to the U.S. Senate, no one worries me more than Michael McLaughlin." http://www.lowellsun.com/todaysheadlines/ci_226192 51/decision-day-mike-mclaughlin#ixzz4QkvIEHY2
5. From the Movie *Rocky*, May 23, 2012 · Rocky and Mickey begin training, but it soon becomes apparent Rocky is lacking motivation. Adrian's brother, Paulie, confronts his sister about not supporting Rocky and

Adrian in turn encourages him to win the fight with this famous quote "Win Rocky Win".

6. *Lawrence Eagle Tribune*, Turnpike Street, North Andover, MA; November 5, 2003.

7. An article; <u>Do negative political ads work</u> published by Scientific American by Donald Green, Professor of Political Science, Columbia University. <u>https://www.scientificamerican.com/article/do-negative-political-ads-work/</u>

8. *Lawrence Eagle Tribune*, Turnpike Street, North Andover, MA; September 18, September 28, October 31, November 2, November 5, 2003.

9. *Lawrence Eagle Tribune*, Turnpike Street, North Andover, MA; November 2, 1993.

10. A "**perfect storm**" is an expression that describes an event where a rare combination of circumstances will aggravate a situation drastically. The term is also used to describe an actual phenomenon that happens to occur in such a confluence, resulting in an event of unusual magnitude. wikipedia.org/wiki/Perfect storm

11. *The Methuen Journal*, November 9, 1993 Volume 2, Number 28 Pages 1, 18, and 19.

12. https://en.wikipedia.org/wiki/Political_capital; Political capital refers to the trust, goodwill, and influence a politician has with the public and other political figures. This goodwill is a type of invisible <u>currency</u> that politicians can use to mobilize the voting public or spend on policy reform.[1] Some thinkers distinguish between reputational and representative political capital. Reputational capital refers to a

politician's credibility and reliability. This form of capital is accumulated by maintaining consistent policy positions and ideological views. Representative capital refers to a politician's influence in policy-setting. This form of capital is accumulated through experience, seniority, and serving in leadership positions.[2] Thus, political capital—reputational and representative—is the product of relationships between opinion (public impressions), policy (legislative rewards/penalties), and political judgment (prudent decision-making).[3]

13. "Leaders are made, they are not born. They are made by hard effort, which is the price which all of us must pay to achieve any goal that is worthwhile".
    Read more at:
    https://www.brainyquote.com/quotes/authors/v/vince_lombardi.html
14. America's Mayor;
    https://en.wikipedia.org/wiki/Rudy_Giuliani_during_the_September_11_attacks
15. http://www.massmoments.org/moment.cfm?mid=355
    Boston Globe, December 12, 13, 14, 1995; September 14, 2003; January 29 and July 27, 2004. *Lawrence Eagle Tribune*, December 12, 1996.
16. Planners Web / New & Information for Citizen Planners Part 1: What Is a Form-Based Code? - Planners Web plannersweb.com/2014/12/fbc1
17. From the movie *Scent of a Woman (1992) - Quotes - IMDb* www.imdb.com/title/tt0105323/quotes Lt. Co. Frank Slade (retired) utters these words to the disciplinary committee at the Baird School Scent of a

Woman (1992) ... You hold this boy's future in your hands, committee. It's a valuable future. Believe me. Don't destroy it. Protect it. Embrace it.

18. Councilor Chuck Turner
https://en.wikipedia.org/wiki/Chuck_Turner

19. *Lawrence Eagle Tribune*, Turnpike Street, North Andover, MA; November 4, 1987 and January 12, 1988.

20. *The Methuen Journal*, January 26, 1994 Volume 2, Number 39 Pages 13.

21. Boston Public Schools - Wikipedia
https://en.wikipedia.org/wiki/Boston_Public_Schools

22. Boston.com *Boston Globe*: On injury leave, firefighter stood out as bodybuilder by W. Robinsonhttp://archive.boston.com/news/local/articl es/2008/07/14/on_injury_leave_firefighter_stood_out _as_bodybuilder/

23. Dr. Barry Bluestone dean of the School of Social Science, Urban Affairs, and Public Policy at Northeastern University. Op-Ed piece entitled "A Future for Public Unions".
http://archive.boston.com/bostonglobe/editorial_opin ion/oped/articles/2009/07/18/a_future_for_public_u nions/

24. U.S. Department of Justice, Wednesday September 30, 2015, https://www.justice.gov/usao-ma/pr/teamsters-indicted-attempted-extortion-reality-television-production-company-0

210

25. *Boston Globe*, September 7,1988 TEACHERS IN LOWELL, PEABODY SET STRIKE REOPENING CANCELED IN LOWELL AFTER VOTE, by Sean Murphy

26. Total Quality Management, https://en.wikipedia.org/wiki/Total_quality_management

27. https://en.wikipedia.org/wiki/Lame_duck_(politics)

28. *Lawrence Eagle Tribune*, Turnpike Street, North Andover, MA; March 2, 1999.

29. *Lawrence Eagle Tribune*, Turnpike Street, North Andover, MA; March 17, 1999.

30. *Lawrence Eagle Tribune*, Turnpike Street, North Andover, MA; October 3, 1998.

31. *Lawrence Eagle Tribune*, Turnpike Street, North Andover, MA; December 27, 1999.

32. *Portland Press Herald* http://www.pressherald.com/2013/01/27/are-24-hour-shifts-more-expensive_2013-01-27/ by Randy Billings.

33. *Lawrence Eagle Tribune*, Turnpike Street, North Andover, MA; December 4, 1998.

34. [PDF]Levy Limits: A Primer on Proposition 2 ½ - Mass.Gov www.mass.gov/dor/docs/dls/publ/misc/levylimits.pdf